THE LAST 42

THE LAST 42

STEVE MELIA

With
PAUL BRAOUDAKIS

The Last 42. Copyright © 2016 by Steve Melia. All rights reserved. No part of this book may be reproduced or transmitted in any form or by any means without written permission from the author.

www.162yankeegames.com

Edited by Paul Braoudakis
Cover Design by Jayce Schmidt

Published by 162 Productions

FIRST Edition

ISBN 978-0-9892123-1-1

Printed in the United States of America.

Dedications

The Last 42 is a tribute to my older brother, James Joseph Melia. 2/5/1966 - 8/2/2013

In January of 2014 I was reminded once again that life is short when beloved Bleacher Creature Udi Laterre left us suddenly. I only knew him short time, but he was one of my favorites fixtures and people at the stadium. He was known for his quick wit, stiff drinks and constant photo bombs. Thanks man, RIP.

Timmy Melia - My Godson and nephew who was a hero as a fireman, marine, and especially a dad. We miss you bud.

To the memory of Sean Webb, A great friend and funny comedian.

A special thanks to the memory of The Great Dave Savula. Dave was the top income earner in LegalShield and will always live in the hearts and minds of associates everywhere. In our business he was the greatest.

Acknowledgments

Mike Melia — What can I say? Thanks for the last 22 years and always having my back.

To those who knew and loved Jim, I hope you find some solace in *The Last 42*.

To Machelle, Daniel, Nick, Cecelia, Josh, and Emily, thanks for making Jim's life fulfilling.

Rick Fleming and to those in the Wildcat Nation at West Shore, thanks for making such a positive impact on Jim's life. Thanks for letting us know how much he meant to you.

To all of his students, parents, and colleagues, please carry Jim's legacy forward.

Danny Melia, Maureen Galvin, and Annie and Katie Melia, thanks for letting me crash at your place for those six weeks.

To my sister Mary and her husband Steve Hamburger, thanks for always being there for me and being a huge part of my life. I miss you!

To Kim Melia, thanks for being there for me when Jim died. It meant a lot.

Matt Dunphy, I am very proud of you.

Macie Grace - I love you so much.

Tom and Lucy Melia, Eileen and Michael McElwee, Geri Soulliere, Marybeth Longona, Trish Nichols, Darryl Campbell, Jorge Tobar, David McElwee, Wayne Stevens, Jim Blakemore, Joey D, Wayne Townsend, Ashley Rice, Jen Quigley, Marilyn and Terry Blair, Rob and Charlene Mackenzie, Chip and Michelle Humphrey, John Busch, Dia Lautenschlager, Patti and Randy Stoltz, Brad and Moire Roberts, Bob and Vicki Levy, Sherranda and Jenkins Ivy, Steve Baker, Tom and Lyse McDonough, Bob and Denny Sappington, Randy and Char Parker, Danielle Detorre, Bonny Jones, Daniel Phoung, Danny and Shauna Vulin, Anita Sarda, Marc Trinidad, Bill and Michelle Guyther, Jorge Tobar, Al Berger, Ferg's Sports Bar, Mark Ferguson, Jeb Apostolakis, Keith and Amelia Wann, Steve and Tina Ferrarra, Scott Opel, Lora Powell, John and Cheryl Ziemblicki, Georgia Makris Taje-Driver, Ben and Lauren Bradshaw, Jimmy Assad, Mike Rezmer, Tony Berni, Danny Trenipohl, Blake Bishop, Sara Newcombe, Annette Terry, Kelli Keys, Judy Tierney, Benito Armenta and all my friends at The Tilted Kilt San Diego, Sportsnet, Greg S. Reid, Marty Appel, Ed Randall, and Brandon Luck.

A Big thanks to Vinny Milano and George Brew, Becki Schick, "Motorcyle" Pete Anderson, Junior Pagan, Jimmy Jenson, Chris Gager and all of the fans around Yankee Stadium for embracing me.

A special shout out to Becca, Louis and all of my

friends at The Dugout

To my friends and associates in LegalShield. Always remember to live YOUR dreams. We have a mission to accomplish. The more we all do, the more freedom we can all create. Work hard and play harder. Life is short. Enjoy it. To my friends on The Platinum Counsel — We are just getting started.

Jeff Bell - Thanks for the joining the team as our CEO. I am grateful for your unwavering quest for greatness and being an amazing leader, friend (BFF), and workout partner.

Paul Braoudakis, thanks for all your help with *The Last 42*!

Jayce - Thanks again for your amazing cover.

To all my comic friends — especially at Dead Crow Comedy — who have the guts to get on stage and make people laugh. Thanks for inspiring me.

Foreword

Having had the great good fortune to hang around THE BEST GAME EVER INVENTED, Steve Melia's story is one of the most heartwarming I have ever heard of. This tribute took a lot more effort than merely scattering the ashes of a loved one over a favorite baseball field.

In tribute to his brother, Steve chose instead to pay tribute by watching his beloved New York Yankees and Mariano Rivera. And then watching them again…
and again…and again…and again…and again…
and again…and again…and again…and again…
and again…and again…and again…and again…
and again…and again…and again…and again…
and again…and again…and again…and again…
and again…and again…and again…and again…
and again…and again…and again…and again…
and again…and again…and again…and again…
and again…and again…and again…and again…and
again…and again…and again…and again…and again

That's 42.

So read this book…42 times.

There'll be a test.

— Ed Randall
    Host of *Ed Randall's Talking Baseball*

CONTENTS

Foreword i
Introduction 15
"It's About Jim ..." 19
There's No Crying in Baseball 29
Life is Theater 43
The 162 Experience 65
The Sausage King, the Peddler Nazi,
  and other Oddities 83
Searching for Denzel 115
How's Your Ass? 137
Perfect Pitch 157
Mo Sets the Tone 183
Creature Features 193
Random Axe of Kindness 205
Boston Strong 221
Flat Screens in Heaven 239
The Tipping Point 265
There *is* Crying in Baseball 291
Epilogue 325
About the Author 329

Introduction

28,000 DAYS

We live an an average of 28,000 days and we never know which one will be our last. For my brother Jim Melia, his last was August 2nd, 2013. He fell well below the average at 17,334, not including leap years. I write this book to celebrate his life and the days that we had with him.

Some of you may know that I claim to be the world record-holder as a fan for consecutive MLB games at 176. In 2011, I decided to fulfill a dream and attend all 162 games of my favorite team, the NY Yankees. Yes, home and away.

I attended the playoffs, as they lost in five games to the Detroit Tigers. I then attended the first nine games of 2012 just to pad my record. That was my favorite year for reasons that went way beyond baseball games. As fun as it was to see Jeter chase 3,000 hits and Mariano

Rivera break Trevor Hoffman's saves record (602), that was really just part of it.

Setting a crazy goal and hitting it was fulfilling. The best part, though, was writing 162 and sharing all of my favorite stories, new friends, and crazy experiences with the reader. Nothing makes me happier then when I get a text, Facebook message, or a kind word from someone who read my book and took the journey with me. If it inspired someone else to live a dream, all the better!

If you assumed that I like baseball, you'd be right. I mostly love the adrenaline rush of attending live events. I recently attended Game 7 of the 2016 NBA Finals and watched Lebron James steal a championship from the record-setting Golden State Warriors. I love the adrenaline rush. I can't enough. Whether it be Game 7 or seeing the Grateful Dead on New Year's Eve, I can't enough of the energy. As a stand up comic and a professional speaker, I get that same feeling from taking the stage and delivering a punchline or a powerful message.

My name is Steve and I'm a fanatic.

In Spring Training of 2013, Mariano Rivera announced that he would retire and that it would be his last season of his Hall off Fame career. I had already been to 21 away games over the first half of the 2013 season. I felt like I was missing one of the biggest sendoffs in MLB history for the greatest closer of all time.

I would catch a game in a loud bar in North Carolina or a hotel room somewhere, but it wasn't the same as being there. With my 162 book published, I was looking for a new project. Mariano was calling out to me.

When my older brother passed suddenly at 47, I decided to keep living every day like it could be my last. I decided to attend the last 42 games.

The Last 42 is a tribute to two men who made an indelible impact on my life and the world. I didn't get to say goodbye to Jim. At least this way I would get a chance to say goodbye to Mariano for the remainder of his illustrious Hall of Fame career.

I have been very blessed as an entrepreneur in that I have created time and financial leverage. This simply means that I have set up in advance my income and it doesn't necessarily need me being there. As a Platinum Council member with LegalShield, I have time freedom to explore my passions.

That's the how and the why. I hope that you enjoy the journey as much as I did.

Chapter One

"IT'S ABOUT JIM ..."

Friday, August 2, 2013

"Hurry, the bus is about to leave."

This a text that Kim sends me. Kim turned 40 a few months back, just after our divorce was finalized.

My brother Mike and I were furiously waving at the bus as we hurried out of the lobby of the famed Opryland Hotel in Nashville, TN. The door squeaked open and we walked on to the many cheers and jeers as the luxury coach whisked us away.

We were at our annual summer retreat with our LegalShield team and headed to The Wild Horse Saloon. There was a buzz in the air. LegalShield, as a newly-branded company, was now two years old and people were excited. These weekends were a blast and we looked forward to them all year. Mike and I grabbed the last two seats on the bus. Kim and my friend Steve Baker were directly behind us. Kim gave Mike and I a fist pump.

We pulled up to the Wild Horse Saloon and piled out in single file. The group was escorted past the long line gathered on the street and we climbed the stairs to the second floor that we have rented out. I made my way up to the bar and took Kim's drink order. I looked behind me and scanned the room for Mike, but didn't see him.

"Where'd my brother go?" I shouted over the loud country music.

"I don't see him. I don't think he ever made it in," Kim said with a shrug as she looked around. *Strange*, I thought, *he was right behind me*. This continued for five minutes as I asked a handful of others from the bus if they saw him. After a few minutes, I semi-frantically made my way down the stairs and out to the street and approached three Nashville Police officers.

"Have you guys seen a guy about 20 years older than me out here? He was just with us and he just seems to have disappeared. No one has seen him." No luck.

I went upstairs again as everyone else was beginning to enjoy the party and the live music. I had a really bad feeling. I texted him. I called him. This was not like

Mike. At first I was just worried that he had to wait in the long line to get in. I went back down and walked through the line asking if anyone had seen him while I used my phone to show his picture. Two burly bouncers were kind enough to stop and listen, but no one had seen him.

Kandra King, a good friend and top sales producer, pulled me aside and said that someone told her that Mike was dealing with a family emergency. My mind raced to his four adult children, aged 27-37. I tried to stay positive as my nephews and nieces all flashed through my mind. Totally stumped after my third trip downstairs, I rejoined the group and took a first sip of my Red Bull and vodka. I made my way to the buffet and filled up a plate. I rejoined Kim at our high-top table.

"Mike's calling me!" Kim said, looking down at her cell. She quickly bolted away from the high-top in search of a quieter location. She made her way to the stairwell in the far corner of the bar. I looked at my plate and my intuition warned me that this might be my last bite of food before hearing some horrible news. I gave Kim a minute and then decided to see what was going on. I swallowed my one bite of dinner, grabbed my drink, and made my way to the stairwell entrance that I saw Kim dart into.

Something was very wrong.

The minute I opened the door to the stairwell and saw her face, I knew that someone was seriously hurt ... or even worse. I knew her well enough to read her face and see the pain immediately. I come from such a huge family, so I was lost as to who or what it might be. A thousand bad scenarios continued to flash through my mind.

"He's right here. I'll tell him," Kim said with a shaky voice while tears streamed down her face.

"What?" I half-heartedly demanded, even though deep down inside I really didn't want to know, whatever it was.

"It's about Jim ... he had a heart attack 45 minutes ago ... he's dead."

"No!"

I started sobbing immediately and uncontrollably as I couldn't even breathe. Jim was my 47-year-old brother. He was a father of five, full of life, and a very well liked and respected educator.

I spent most of the next few hours in the stairwell going through the first stages of grief as many of my friends came to offer their thoughts, consoling words, and shots of tequila, which seemed to do nothing to numb my instant pain. Chip Humphrey made his way out. Chip and Jim taught together and Jim recruited Chip into LegalShield. Chip lost his brother tragically years ago and could relate at a deep level. He and I were hugging and crying. Everyone was shocked and saddened.

When I awoke the next morning, my very first conscious thought was me praying that last night was just a horrible nightmare. It wasn't. So this was Day One without my big brother. Simply surreal.

I was scheduled to have coffee at 8 a.m. with the president of our company, Alan Fearnley. Kim texted Mike and me and told us that she would take care of it. I spent the morning crying while reading Facebook posts from Jim's students and friends. In our new world of social media, news spread quickly. Mike and I skipped the seminar that we were supposed to be running. Even though Kim was every bit as upset as us, she courageously represented the Melia Family.

John Hoffman is a friend of 20 years and top leader in our company. We were co-running this event with 500 associates from all over the U.S. and Canada. John opened up with a moment of silence as the crowd respectfully bowed and prayed. Chip also stood up and had a chance to talk about Jim during the session as well. We didn't see or hear any of this firsthand as we both stayed confined to our hotel rooms directly next to each other.

We were now seven siblings down to six. Mike spent the morning calling around to the rest of our family. My sister

Jim and I looking cool with jackets slung over our shoulders.

Mary and her husband Steve, along with my brother Tommy and his wife Lucy, were in Ireland on a six-week vacation of a lifetime. They were the only ones we couldn't reach. Mike reached Danny the previous night as he was walking home from a bar in Long Island with his wife Maureen after celebrating their anniversary. Mike also reached our sister Eileen as she was in a hotel room in Savannah on her way back home to Florida. She and Jim were very close. In fact, he died in the kitchen of the house that she sold Jim and his wife Machelle.

Like any stereotypical Irish Catholic brothers, we eventually moved the event to one of the many bars in Opryland. Mike and I recalled story after story about

Big Jim. Jim was the largest of the Melia clan, standing at 6' 6". He was a star high school basketball player at Vero Beach High School, proudly capturing the MVP award both his junior and senior year in 1983 and 1984. I would only miss one of his games if my junior high team had a game the same night. I idolized Jim and how popular and well liked he was in high school. I would throw his name around whenever I could.

By mid-afternoon we had reached everyone with the news. It was hard telling his friends. Mike made most of the really tough calls. Me and my brother and business partner of nearly 20 years were bellied up to the bar laughing one moment and crying the next. We were in stunned disbelief. Despite the mental fog, I had a moment of crystal clarity as an idea popped into my head while I held up a copy of *162*, which I self-published four months earlier.

"I know what I'm going to do next ... to honor Jim," I confidently announced. My older brother looked up from his Shiner Bock.

"I have the idea for my next book," I proclaimed. "I'm going to call it *The Last 42: Life is Short, Enjoy the Journey*." I started it as a question, but I completed it as a statement. I passionately laid out the vision for my new quest, which would be to attend the last 42 games of Mariano Rivera's career.

Mariano's number is 42 and he is the last major leaguer

to display that number. 42 is the only number to ever be retired throughout all of baseball and was done so to honor the late Jackie Robinson. Mo (Rivera's nickname that I will be using frequently throughout the book) and 13 others still donned that number when it was retired. Major League Baseball allowed them to keep wearing it while they played, but no new number 42's would be issued. That edict was given in 1997. Sixteen years later, Mo was the last 42 ... and he was in the midst of one of the biggest sendoffs in MLB history.

Mike quickly pulled out his iPhone to check the schedule and count the games backwards to see where the last 42 games would begin.

"You got 13 days," he announced dryly.

Oh, jeesh.

We walked through the schedule. Compared to 2011, this should be a can of corn. The first game would be at Fenway Park on August 16th. The season ended in Houston on September 29th. Because I am one of the few fans who have ever done all 162 games, I knew that it was possible. I was relieved to discover that I could even drive or take trains to most of the remaining games.

To myself, my brother Jim, and to the rest of the world's baseball fans, Mariano Rivera was a complete stud — the total package. He exemplified great character, professionalism, and had a reputation of treating everyone with class and dignity. Those words also perfectly described my brother Jim. This book — this quest — would be a way to honor two great men.

Later that evening, we did a live auction to raise funds for our charity, "Work, Play, Love." I was supposed to host and be the auctioneer, but couldn't muster up the energy to do it. The Vice President of Sales, Tony Petrill, filled in and hosted with another great friend, Cliff Malloy of New York. I didn't even want to be at the event. I didn't want to accept everyone's condolences. It made it too real and there were lots of people there that I barely knew. In some sense it seemed fake. I only wanted to be around my family and closest of friends.

We were escorted into the live auction before the doors opened to the group. There were numbers on sticks scattered about as we were supposed to grab one for the auction. I quickly found 162 and also grabbed 42. I had Mike snap a picture. Kim came over and asked "Are you really going to do it?" I told her I would as long as I had her buy-in. We raised more than $15K that night, but I was too numb to appreciate it. After the auction, Kim hung out in my room and prepared a cucumber facial to help reduce the swelling around my eyes.

The next morning we had a breakout session where our team got together for a weekend wrap-up and to plan out the next three to four months as an organization. We had roughly 200 people seated classroom-style in the hotel ballroom. An hour in, I stood up and shared my favorite Jim Melia stories. Kim continued to be a rock. Mike was having a hard time as he got up to leave the room several times.

This was our team and if I was going to write a new book and take the next six weeks going to baseball games to do it, this was the group that I wanted to announce it to. This was —and is — the team that makes it all happen. Most of them aren't even baseball fans, so I spent a few minutes setting it up. I talked about Jackie Robinson and Mariano Rivera and what they meant to the game of baseball. Then I announced that beginning August 16 I would be attending the last 42 games of the year and — more importantly — Mariano's career.

I had no idea at the time, but this journey was going to be about so much more than baseball.

Chapter Two

THERE'S NO CRYING IN BASEBALL

The funeral and memorial service for Jim had been slated for the weekend of August 8-9. For the past couple of days, I had become addicted to checking Facebook to see what others were posting about Jim. Pictures, stories, and testimonials were flowing in. It was impossible to make it through a session without crying. It had only been three days.

Kindness, fairness, encouraging, caring and *gentle* were the words that I saw most often. The words from family and friends alike were affirming of a life well-lived.

> *It is with great sadness that I reflect upon the life and times of Big Jim, my younger brother who passed suddenly on Friday evening.*
>
> *Those of you who knew him would agree that he was a Gentle Giant. To write of him in the past tense is totally surreal for me.*

Please keep his wife Machelle and their five wonderful kids in your prayers. Thanks to everybody for your love and your messages. I appreciate each of you. Take care of and appreciate your loved ones. See greatness in them.

- Mike Melia

I'm living under a cloud of shock and sadness today, knowing that my uncle Jim Melia is suddenly gone, dead of a heart attack way too young. He was a gentle giant, with an aptitude for asking the question you needed to hear. He was a teacher, coach and school administrator, and it's been both sad and soothing to see his students posting about the positive impact he made on their lives.

I'll miss you, Uncle Jim. I wish you had a few decades more to do your thing.

-Luke Melia

Thank you so much to all of my friends and Jim Melia's friends who have reached out today about my brother's passing. Just like Jim, I am truly blessed to be surrounded by so many great people who care about me. Today was tough. Please keep his wife Machelle and his five beautiful children in your thoughts. I had the honor of being the best man at Jim and Machelle's wedding.

He was simply a helluva nice of a guy with a huge heart and an encouraging word for all. I feel lucky to have had him for a big brother for my 43 years.

> He certainly made me a better person and inspired me to think bigger. Jim and I moved to Sebastian, Florida with my parents in 1978. We were two fish out of water when we moved from Long Island. Jim went on to be a star high school basketball player. He was named MVP Jr. and Sr. year. After graduating from FSU decided to make a difference in the classroom and as a coach.
>
> He was a teacher by nature; inside and outside of the classroom. He was always curious about how and why things worked. It is evident from all of his former students comments that Jim reached his goal of making a positive difference. I'll miss him. I already do. You made the world a much better place. See you on the other side brother.
>
> **-Steve Melia**

This was the statement that West Shore Principal Rick Fleming sent out:

> "It is with a heavy heart and soul that I report to you that our beloved Mr. Jim Melia passed away on Friday night due to an apparent heart attack. Naturally, the Nation is grieving as a result of this tremendous and sudden loss to our school as Mr. Melia was somewhat of an icon to our entire school community. He was feared by most but loved by all and his jovial spirit and personality will be sincerely missed. At the moment we are still quite numb over this loss as is his immediate family therefore no arrangements have been announced as of yet. Please keep Mr. Melia's family in your thoughts and

prayers.

As we all grapple and grieve through this in our own way I wanted to let everyone know that we will have grief counselors on hand during registration and for the start of the school year to assist any in our school community who may need it. Mr. Melia embodied everything West Shore is ... hard work, family, fellowship, and commitment and this loss is obviously hard to take for all of us. In spite of the loss however I know that he would want us to carry on in true Wildcat fashion by preparing for yet another positive and productive school year.

Thank you in advance for your compassion, your patience, and your collective understanding during this difficult time."

Sincerely,

Rick Fleming, Principal

And this came from one of his players/students.

Wow!!! RIP Coach Melia. Man!!! You touched and mentored so many of us in the game of life and basketball. I remember my 7th grade year at SRMJHS during basketball tryouts you told me, "Dudley next year you have to learn how to do a left-handed layup and you need to be stronger." So that whole summer I practiced my layups and I did push ups. During tryouts that next year you pulled me in front of the team and said, "This is what happens when you work hard." I will never forget that or you Coach Melia . One of many awesome memories. God Bless All. Peace, Love and Happiness -

-Smilez Dudley

With the funeral just a couple of days away, I remember lying in bed fully awake at 2:47 a.m. I was full of doubtful thoughts about *The Last 42*. Was I running away ... or celebrating Jim's life? I couldn't shake the thought. Much like Opening Day in 2011, I began to seriously question my new venture. Maybe I was nuts. Could I afford this? All of my commitments ran through my head. Could my business take me losing focus again? How much will this cost? I was having major doubts about my trip. I had a lot of things going on in my life.

Mike, Jim, and me.

I went down to the hotel's continental breakfast, broke out my journal, and did a "Ben Franklin." This is an exercise when you list all of the pros and cons to help make a better decision.

PROS	CONS
This will be a great way to keep Jim's spirit alive.	Some of my responsibilities back home will suffer (house, bills, etc.).
This could be an opportunity to inspire millions of more people that can be positively affected because of Jim and his life lessons.	Being on the road is hard on the body and the wallet.
I can say goodbye to Mariano, like I didn't get to do for Jim.	The Yankees are having their worst season in years and a playoff berth looks slim.

PROS	CONS
Attending Mariano Rivera's last 42 games will be really fun.	Maybe I am running away from my problems.
The Last 42 will really help me promote *162*.	
Life is short — The trip will be therapeutic.	

The next day, the Yanks lost again 3-2 for their fifth straight game. As I considered my decision, I could see Jim's big frame asking me, "Is it really about the wins and losses or is it about honoring Mariano?"

"It's more about doing something special to remember you, Big Guy," is how I would have responded.

I crammed into a booth with my girlfriend Ashley who lived in Chicago. We were at an Asian-themed restaurant and finished up by cracking open a fortune cookie. It read:

You have a charming way with words and should write a book.

Hmm.

As most fortune cookies do, they usually post some "lucky numbers" on the backside of the fortune. The numbers on the back were: 7, 19, 26, 32, 34, 42.

I added them up. Am I going crazy? They equal 162. And the last number in the sequence is 42.

That's all I needed to see. Thank you, Universe.

So the decision was confirmed. I would be attending the last 42 games of the 2013 season.

Later, while in the shower preparing for the evening's game, I broke down and just lost it. An overwhelming cloud of grief came over me and whacked me in the head like a two-by-four. I dropped and just sat in the tub, sobbing. For five minutes I just let it all out and cried uncontrollably. I didn't have the energy to stand, so I just sat limply in the hotel tub and let the shower wash away my tears. In the days and weeks to come, crying in the shower became part of my daily routine.

The game that evening was my 21st game of the year, all of which had been away games. We were at Bacardi at the Park across from U.S. Cellular Field in Chicago. I partied here during my *162* tour and they were nice enough to let me set up my books on the outside patio. I had sold out the *162* "Rockstar Package" tickets and had 40 friends and fans coming out that evening. The

Rockstar Package was for those who purchased the book and wanted to attend a game with me in their city.

As the Rockstars arrived, I was met with hugs from most and tears from others. Amazingly, all 40 showed up, even though a massive thunderstorm rolled in around 4 p.m. As I signed the books and snapped pictures, other fans come over and learned of my journey. I sold another 15 books residually to the fans at Bacardi.

The Yanks were leading going into the ninth inning, 4-3. Mariano Rivera came in for his last appearance in Chicago. I did my best to explain the relevance to some of the more novice fans around me. I was the most excited person in my section as I was able to escape reality for a few hours and cheer for the Yankees legend.

With two outs, Mariano gave up three straight hits and blew the lead. The Sox tied it 4-4. Mo proved that he is human. The Yanks fought back to take the lead again in the 12th with an Alfonzo Soriano homerun. Well, at least we are leaving on a positive note ... or so I thought. A few short minutes later, the Sox rallied for two additional runs and walked away with a win. I was really being tested as the 27-time world champs got swept by one of the worst teams in baseball!

To add to the misery, Alex Rodriguez and 12 other players were suspended the day before. Alex's 212-

game suspension was the stiffest and would last the remainder of the season and the entire 2014. Rodriguez was the only player to appeal. He had been injured all year and was making his 2013 debut this evening in Chicago. The timing sure is interesting.

His appeal would allow him to continue to play until a hearing, which would not be until after the season. So, arguably the greatest player of his time was in the lineup for the game on this night. The stadium rocked with fans booing, screaming, and just saying nasty things about the 38-year-old who already has self-esteem issues.

Dads shared with their sons how A-Rod is a cheater and has set the wrong example. Others yelled that he should take his punishment like a man. Every nickname imaginable was yelled and put in Sharpies on signs. "A-Roid," "Juicer," "A-Fraud." I am an observer, not a protester.

A Yankees fan seated close to me pointed out that it was ironic that White Sox fans were so irate over cheating. Those not familiar with baseball history may have missed that the "Black Sox" of 1919 threw the World Series. Yep, they took bribes to lose on purpose. Hmm. Good point and well played.

But these fans sprung for the tickets for this game and they wanted to boo, so let them boo.

Thursday, August 8

> *I've been on here a gazillion times, begin to write and fall completely apart. I'm devastated. There is now another hole in my heart and I'll never be "Wholehearted" again. You've been a source of love, friendship, guidance and strength to me for, OMGH 30 YEARS! Our paths have intertwined throughout our lives and I will always love you and completely cherish our special friendship. I promise to carry on your message "It all begins in the classroom!"*
>
> *Georgia Makris Taje-Driver*

Jim's longtime friend, Georgia, emailed me and asked if it would be all right to start a foundation and name it in honor of Jim. I was on a plane for Melbourne, FL. I had taken many trips to the Sunshine State over the last 20 years. I was not only sad, but there were knots in my stomach. It had only been six days without my older brother, but it seemed like a lifetime.

My sister Mary and brother Tommy were flying in from Europe. Kim was flying in from California. Many of Jim's friends were traveling in as well. My sister Eileen called and asked me to do the eulogy. I was honored, but nervous. In fact, I considered this the biggest honor and privilege of my life. Jim made such an impact on those around him that and I wanted to do a good job in communicating that. One of Jim's sons, Nick, wrote a beautiful piece that I was asked to read at the funeral.

Mike picked me up from the airport and I twisted his arm to stop at Hiram's Tiki Bar in Sebastian, a favorite watering hole for a few decades. Sitting at the outside bar was Mike Rezmer. Rez came in from Orlando and was one of Jim's best friends. He was taking it as hard as we were. Within a few hours, five more of Jim's old buddies arrived and commenced around a table sharing stories and cocktails. I knew most of them pretty well, but hadn't seen them in 15 years. They were all five-plus years older than me and I idolized many of them in high school. It was great to hear them speaking so highly of the Big Guy. Everyone still seemed to be in shock. There were as many laughs as tears as stories from the glory days were revealed and shared.

By dusk there were 30 people there. The impromptu gathering was full of laughs and tears. More friends kept rolling in. It was really pretty cool. I personalized a few *162* books and distributed them to several of Jim's closest friends. I used to sign the books, "Live your dreams." I now added, "Life is short – Enjoy the journey."

Around 8:30, Kim showed up. It says a lot about Kim that she would fly from California for her ex's husband's brother's funeral. Along with her was the crew from Europe. They all met and rented a car in Orlando after their arduous overseas trip. My sister Mary and brother Tommy were the second and third siblings I had seen since Jim's death. From seven down to six. We are a tight family and it was a little easier with each other to lean on, but maybe more difficult because of our closeness.

Friday, August 9

This day rolled around so quickly. It was hard to believe it had already been a week. It was a miserable week to be sure, but one that was ironically full of joy as well. The joy stemmed from the reaction and outpouring of love from Jim's community.

We had a 10 a.m. viewing of the body for the family only. It was tough to see his face one last time. Maybe because he had been dead for a week, but I think they did a horrible job in preparing him for the viewing.

Machelle, Jim's wife of nearly nine years showed up and she looked absolutely devastated. As much as Jim was a big guy at 6' 6", she was tiny at barely 5' 3". I hugged her, but understandably she didn't have the strength to even put any energy into it. Four of their five kids could not bear to even be there. Seeing the body was too much. Nick, a freshmen at FSU, was there to support his mom, but stood in the back of the funeral parlor.

"I read your letter," I told him. "It was well written and very powerful."

"Thanks. Jim meant a lot to us," he replied softly.

"I am totally prepared to read it for you," I offered, "but as the time gets closer, if you change your mind and feel that you are up for it, let me know."

Down the road, I know that Nick would be glad he did.

One by one my relatives arrived and paid their respects. We sat around and shared what Jim meant to us and whatever was on our minds. We laughed as often as we cried. That seemed to be the theme. Another thing that we all agreed on is that Jim was taken from us way too early.

While the funeral parlor we were in represented death, there was still a world out there and lots of life still left to be lived. There were a slew of dreams, goals, and visions that still needed to be lived out.

My mind kept going to the mountain of logistics and details that I needed to handle to get ready for *The Last 42*. I could almost hear my big brother saying, "Go get it done!"

And who was I to argue with Big Jim?

Chapter Three

LIFE IS THEATER

Eileen had arranged for some friends from church to host the entire family at her home. We relaxed by the pool as I shared my Last 42 idea with the family. No one seemed very surprised by it. In fact, they were all very supportive. Tom and Lucy were headed back to Europe and would be gone for most of the rest of the season. I stayed with them for the majority of home games in 2011. They were awesome to live with and gracious.

My brother and FDNY Battalion Chief Danny Melia and his wife Maureen live in Rockville Center. I texted them a few days prior and asked them if I could stay with them for the Last 42. They talked and said they would love to have me. With Jim's passing, the idea of hanging out with them was comforting.

We were due at the memorial service at 6 p.m. at the

Cocoa Village Playhouse theater. Jim volunteered there often and many of his five children had performed in countless plays there. I was immediately overwhelmed as we walked down the street and saw a line gathering. We walked by easily 100 people and knocked on the door. Someone let us in and we were escorted to the front of this huge theater. There was a giant picture of Jim on what must have been a 30-foot screen. It read *Jim Melia 2/6/1966–8/2/2013*. Just like in all of his pictures, he was wearing a huge smile.

Over the next 10 minutes, I was brought to tears and filled with pride as people just keep coming and coming. The main floor filled quickly as the 350 seats were all taken. The balcony began to fill up as well. By the time the ceremony started there were more than 500 in attendance to celebrate the life of my big brother. There were also dozens of students and actors backstage rehearsing for the event.

The production began with a lady who was in charge of the playhouse. She opened up and shared what a big impact Jim had on the theater and how his presence as a volunteer always made a big difference. She relayed that his huge frame seemed like a permanent fixture in the back of the theater for all of the rehearsals and performances. She went on to describe a person who had a secret passion for show tunes. He either hid this from me or I just never paid attention. I looked at my brothers and sisters with a look that said, "Are they talking about *Jim*?" The program continued as the cast from different productions belted out show tunes. We are treated to "Phantom of the Opera" and many other classics.

The front row was open and reserved for his family. I'll always remember Machelle and the kids walking in from backstage. The kids looked devastated. The girls especially looked as if they were in a complete fog. Most of my brothers and sisters were in the second row. Kim and I were in the front on the right. I spotted one of Jim's best friends, Danny Trenipohl. I was the one who had to tell him about Jim just a week ago. We both cried like babies. I went to the back and escorted him to an empty seat next to me.

The first of the memorial speakers was Jim's principal and close friend Rick Fleming. When I first heard of Jim's death, I immediately and wrongly blamed Rick. When Jim first got the job, he was not allowed to have any interest in business projects. Jim had been working LegalShield with us part-time for several years. This job as a dean was a great opportunity and he drifted away from working with us. I placed blame because I felt if Jim was more well-balanced and had stuck with personal development that often accompanies the business, he may have been healthier. I realize now that this was just part of the stages of grief and I was looking to place my anger somewhere.

As Rick spoke, I could feel his compassion. He loved Jim. I felt his friendship and it was obvious that they were extremely close. As he continued and shared some great moments about Jim, it became apparent how he represented an entire community that appreciated my brother and would miss him tremendously. He joked how he would sometimes make Jim close the door to his office and iron his shirt. He even threw his tie over his shoulder to mimic Jim. He spoke of how he will always remember Jim's huge frame crammed into his trusty golf cart that he maneuvered around campus. Rick's words were soothing and it became clear that Rick and Jim were more than friends — they were a team. They both cared about their job and, most importantly, the kids who roamed their hallways.

I was floored by the turnout. I constantly turned around to gauge the crowd's reaction as the night progressed. It was amazing to me that all of these people really cared that much. It brought me tremendous comfort. The crowd was laughing and crying along with the families. Of all the places that teenagers could be on a Friday night, they chose to honor an educator. This night would go down as one of the most touching nights of my life.

It was uplifting to know that Jim was going out surrounded by so many lives that he impacted. I had a host of mixed emotions. I almost felt jealous that we had to share our big brother with everyone. This was the most I had ever cried since I was a child. With both of my parents, I spent years preparing for the inevitable. With Jim, it was so unexpected. At other funerals that I have been to, I almost felt like I have to force myself to cry because it is the right thing to do. Not this time. Tears continued to run down my face as the night progressed.

My mind wandered back to the last night that we hung out in Delaware, a month prior. I tried to remember if we even said goodnight or goodbye. Jim left early the next day and that was the last time we would see each other or talk. We went to a very expensive dinner that last night as we were spending the remainder of my dad's inheritance.

Jim ordered the surf and turf, and so did I, as well as my brother Danny and my brother-in-law, Steve Hamburger.

"I've never ordered something without knowing the price," Jim admitted.

"How much could it be?" I remember my sister asking across the table. It turns out it was $49.95.

My last real memory of Jim was us walking back from

dinner and him telling us that it was the best meal he had ever had. I remember how he lit up as he expressed his delight in the meal. Jim was pretty simple and wasn't afraid to tell you when he liked something.

Jim was in charge of discipline at West Shore. He interacted regularly with the school's resource officer. Every school was assigned a police officer that would be present on campus. He worked with Jim for several years and shared what an impact Jim made and was always amazed that Jim knew every single student on campus by name. "He knew all of the parents by name as well," the officer recalled.

My nephew David was a big part of the memorial as he spent many hours at this facility delighting audiences. He was the first of the Melia Clan to get up on stage that night. My brother Danny took the stage next. He and Jim were probably the closest in size as Danny comes in at 6' 3" with big, broad shoulders. He is a FDNY chief in charge of safety. He set the tone for the rest of the night by being both funny and emotional.

I remember back to when we were kids in Florida and Danny was visiting us. He and Jim were always so competitive. Just as Jim was passing Danny in size, they came to blows one night. Jim tackled him in the guest room like Lawrence Taylor as the two of them tumbled through the screened door to the back porch. A few years ago, a similar situation developed where they were arguing on the golf course and it was almost a rematch of the Rocky and Mr. T fight. They were in a sand trap and yelling at the top of their lungs. I thought Jim was going to kill him.

As I watched my brother fighting emotions to best represent the family, I chuckled to myself. *Isn't that what families do?* They fight and then they make up. Especially our family. Danny always does a good job of easing the tension, but still capturing the moment. He was way funnier than expected. I had been to many memorials over the years. We have such a big family and there is usually a time to speak. I remember looking over at Jim on such occasions to see if he was going to get up there. Not this time. Not any time.

When Danny was finished, I mustered up the courage and silently prayed for the strength to pull this off.

"My brother Danny isn't usually that funny," I began. To be honest, that was the last thing that I remember saying. I know that I told a few stories of Jim and how he was my moral compass, but the rest is a blur.

When the production was complete, many of the crowd made their way to the front to console the families. I'll always remember one young man who worked his way through the crowd.

"Your brother and I were very close," he said. "He was sort of a mentor to me. Just so you know, Mr. Melia really looked up to you. He talked nonstop about you and your *162* book. He also bragged how you had the courage to be a stand up comedian. He spoke of you often. He was proud of you."

I thanked him then and I thank him now. That young man didn't have to come up to a complete stranger and attempt to make me feel better. But he did. Maybe he learned that kindness from his family. Maybe he was returning the kindness and gentleness that was shown to him by Jim. Whatever it was, he has no idea how grateful I was by his words. They came at the perfect time.

What was just as amazing was the parents of the students who were also there. One in particular was Rebecca Barney. She pulled me aside and kindly shared how Jim impacted her daughter's life.

This is a letter she wrote to me a few days later on Facebook.

> *Hi Steve.... I'm not one for requesting friends with people I don't really know. I'm not on here to have a record number of friends. I wanted to let you know why I requested you. My daughter went to West Shore and graduated in 2011. She was home last weekend when we she got the news about your brother Jim passing. She came running into my bedroom at 1am after we had returned home from a fun night out together. She was hysterical, in tears telling me she just found out Mr. Melia had died. I could hardly believe the news myself so I called Officer Landmesser, a friend. He confirmed our fear.*

Life is Theater

You see West Shore isn't your average high school. It is more like a family. It's a relatively small school with 900 students in 7th through 12th grade. Our daughter went there all 6 years and loved it for that reason. Your brother Jim was there her entire time. She played basketball and we never missed a game. It was kind of like a dream team of educators at West Shore. You could tell that nearly every teacher and administrator were there because they wanted to be there, not just for a paycheck. Mr. Melia was no different.

There are countless stories we remember of him over those 6 years. I guess for my daughter, one of her most memorable was in 9th grade. She was late for class a few too many times and she got sent down to Jim's office. It was her first time ever being reprimanded for anything so as soon as she walked into his office she started sobbing. She said he calmed her down immediately and talked it over like it was no big deal and before she knew it, she was on her way back to class with a smile. That was the resounding message we have heard about him over the last week. He truly was a blessing and had a gift. It is obvious that teaching and leading were his passion. He made it look so easy. We attended both the memorial and the funeral this past weekend. I must say that I've been to my fair share of them in my 40 yrs and none have been more beautiful and touching than Jim's.

We knew what he was like at West Shore, but obviously, we didn't know him as a brother, father, husband, uncle, son-in-law, brother-in-law. It is evident by all of the testimony from your family and his wife and children that he was an amazing guy in his personal life as well. Anyway, I was really touched by your family. The strength, talent, closeness, and most of all LOVE is something you don't see all too often in families today. I had no idea about your 162 book until you mentioned it when you spoke about Jim. He must have been a humble man as well. Our family are big Red Sox fans and we used to have friendly banter back and forth with Jim and Rick Fleming about our rivalries. He had never mentioned the book. As much as I dislike the Yankees, reading about your experience and dream coming true was extremely cool, captivating and motivating.

After viewing your FB page and website I wanted to continue to follow your journey and experience with The Last 42. In some way it might also make us feel connected to Jim. His passing is a huge loss to our community and to West Shore just as it is to your family. But like you all said, he would want us all to carry on. He truly is a legacy to an amazing school. He is gone now but will never be forgotten. As we sadly sit on our shore and wave goodbye to wonderful man we remember that he has arrived on another shore where there are those waiting, welcoming him home, with love and eternal peace. Godspeed to Jim and all the best of luck to you with The Last 42. Looking forward to following your inspirational journey.

All the best to you.

Sincerely,

Rebecca Barney

I woke up the next morning on the couch in a timeshare that was gifted to us for the weekend. I still hadn't written the final eulogy that I would deliver in two hours. I had some ideas, just nothing solid. I had only been given five minutes, but I knew that I would go way longer than that.

We pulled up to the church and, much like the night before, I was instantly brought to tears at the sight of the full parking lot. There were people everywhere who showed up to pay their respects. I saw friends that I hadn't seen since high school as well as many friends of Jim. I greeted former teachers and saw many people I had forgotten about.

I looked over a sea of people from the back of the church. Most of them I didn't recognize. It hit me that this was the same church where Jim and Machelle got married. That day was filled with joy and tears. On this day, it was mostly tears. My siblings and I were blown away by the number of lives that Jim had touched. I think we all felt that we missed a part of his life. Sometimes with your family, you only know them in a certain way. I felt like I missed how special he was. It could be one of the stages of grief.

One of our neighbors growing up in Sebastian, Alison Basini, made her way through the crowd and gave me a much-needed hug. "I became a teacher because of Jim," she told me. "When I got my first job, I reached out to him and we talked often. He always gave me great advice."

The family stood in the back as we looked over the packed Catholic church. We would walk in together in solidarity. We were a little smaller on this day, but just as strong.

My brother-in-law, Michael McElwee, is a deacon and he walked me through the ceremony. He would be delivering the homily. I made my way over to Nick and he said that he decided he would like read his piece on Jim after all. I smiled. "That's how Jim would have wanted it. You'll do great," I assured him.

I spotted an entire section of Jim's friends, many of whom I hadn't seen in 20 years. I waved and flashed a big smile as I remembered always wanting to hang out with these guys. I also spotted his former teammates, fishing and poker buddies, old girlfriends, neighbors, former students, and hundreds of other faces I didn't recognize. I tried to absorb as much as I could and embrace the moment.

"Can you believe this? Who are these all of these people?" Mary asked bewilderedly. We joked that there was no way any of us would have a funeral this big.

Everyone was here except Mike and his family. I texted him that we were about to start. They raced in just in time as we are being seated. It meant more than words can describe that Kim was there. Jim was always a big fan of Kim's, and after we broke up he would always ask about her.

The service was beautiful as some of my nieces and nephews were included in the mass. I thought back to my mom who passed eight years prior. When I was an altar boy, she would always sit in the front row and try to make eye contact with me during the songs. I smiled as I remembered her favorite, *Peace is Flowing Like a River.*

Nick made his way to the altar and delivered one of the finest tributes imaginable. The young man has the heart of a champion. He worked his way to the front of the room and spoke eloquently.

> *I only had the privilege of knowing Jim for the past decade, but in that time he left a lasting imprint on my family and myself. To look back on a time before Jim is like remembering a past life, because his impact was immediate and lasting. When he first started dating my mother it was like being thrown into the fire that is our family, yet he just seemed to bask in it. Jim took to us immediately and despite our vast differences, found a way to connect with each of us kids. It was not easy at first, but that is just a testament to both his will and his love for our mother. Jim solidified his spot in our family by*

doing all in his power to help us out. Whether it be dropping us off at school, helping write my American history paper, or teaching me a left handed layup, Jim was there to help with it all. In a two-year span, Jim received about 12 years worth of parenting experience, culminating in a marriage to my mother where he earned the right to call himself my parent. While Jim started out with just a spot in our family, he soon turned that into a vital role. He managed to find a way to support us all in one way or another.

If anything could make this tragedy harder to bear it is the fact that Jim was so supportive. In times of sadness and strife, which seemed to come in abundance in our family, Jim was the one who picked us back up. He did so to our entire family when he married my mother and to myself personally on more occasions than I can remember. Jim had the rare ability of making you feel OK after doing something you know was wrong. Helping people remember that they are not defined by single actions, but the choices they make and the person they strive to become. While he may have been an outstanding disciplinarian at West Shore, I must confess that he did not play that role in our house. Jim was not one to yell or speak in anger; instead he provided words of counsel and condolence. You know how most parents don't get mad, they get disappointed? Jim didn't even get disappointed, he would tell me he did worse in his day and was proud that I owned up to my actions like a man.

While Jim's title has a "step" before it, that did not make him any less of a father. A father is someone who drives you to your first peewee football team, sits to watch you practice, and does so every day for the next three years. A father reminds you that at 6th grade you still have time to shed that baby fat, but he would love you the same even if you didn't. A father drives his son to freshman orientation and helps move in to his first apartment. A father aligns the moral compass of his kids letting them know right from wrong. Jim did every single one of these things for me, especially the last. This might be sacrilege, but WWJD always had a slightly different meaning for me.

While grieving is never easy or quick, I am trying and urge others to try, and just remember the wonderful time we were lucky enough to have spent with Jim. Jim will live on the memories of all who knew him, I'd like to take this time and share with you all some of my personal favorites.

I can still remember going to West Shore's summer basketball camp as a kid and learning how to play basketball with him and his players. Turns out basketball is not my sport as I quickly found out, which disappointed me because I wanted to impress Jim at one of his favorite pastimes. Jim saw me sitting on the bench and asked what was wrong, I promptly responded with "I suck," to which he assured me I did not. Upon seeing that consolation was not coming quickly, he said, "Come with me." We snuck out of camp and drove across the causeway to get some ice cream at Del's Freeze. He told me a story of himself and his father, the lesson being that pride comes in the individual and not their actions alone.

Another vivid memory occurred during my senior year of high school and has meant a lot to me. That year, I was finally starting in football, playing every snap on defense. Our team was good the year before, but Jim and I talked of this team being better. I played 11 games that season and whether it was home or away, winning or losing, across the state or down the road, I could look to the stands and see Jim's unmistakable figure. While this might not be a shining achievement for some, remember I am one of five children all with various sports and activities. This was the first time anyone had attended every single one of my games, it gave me such pride knowing that he was sitting there being proud of me. His presence at those games always meant so much, it also helped the team because we won every game that year.

The last sentiment I will share goes back to one of the first times I ever met Jim. As kids we felt it was our duty to test Jim, see if he could handle life with us. We started out by switching our names around and being exceptionally hyperactive, I think one of my siblings even came out with a wig and alter ego of themselves. The point being that night my brother Daniel asked Jim if he wanted to play chess, assuming he could easily beat Jim. Defeat came swiftly for Daniel, followed by myself in the next game, but that night started a tradition of challeng-

> ing Jim at a game of chess. Through the years we played more times than I can count just talking of whatever interested us that particular day or the latest lesson in my AP history class. Each game ended with myself promising to one day be good enough to finally best him in a game of chess.
>
> I apologize for not fulfilling that promise Jim, but I will continue to better myself in your honor; both in chess and in life.

Nick was simply amazing. Jim would have wept like a big baby.

I have been blessed to overcome my fear of public speaking at a young age and have been speaking in front of audiences for 20 years. All of my experiences, I believe, led me to this moment. I took the opportunity to eulogize my brother Jim very seriously. I slowly made my way to the podium and gave it all I had.

> Good morning. Of course, if Jim were here, he would say, "Why are you telling me to have a good morning, when I can have a great morning?"
>
> This has been the most difficult week of my life. However, it has also been one of the most amazing. Thanks to many of you that have expressed what Jim meant to you through Facebook, over the phone, or at the memorial last night. Our family has been able to see a side of Jim that we didn't know existed.
>
> Jim and I often spoke about an article that was writ-

The Last 42

> ten years ago. It stated that the average funeral will have 5-10 people crying. We always reflected that the number of people crying was a good indicator of how you lived your life. It is apparent that he led an outstanding life and judging from the crowd, he was way above average.
>
> Jim's tombstone will read 2/5/1966 – 8/2/2013.
>
> Two of my cousins, Cindy Hall and Debbie Ziemblicki, both posted this poem called "The Dash" earlier this week.

I read the poem by Linda Ellis aloud to the crowd and I barely made it through without my voice cracking. I took a deep breath.

> Jim wasn't only my big brother, but like for many he was my moral compass. I would often make decisions based on whether I would get caught or what the consequences might be. Jim made his decisions on what was the right thing to do. I'll live my life a little differently knowing he's watching over me.
>
> My fondest memories are going to every one of his high school basketball games with my parents. He wore number 52 for Vero Beach High School and was the team MVP his junior and senior years. I was so proud to be his little brother and watched and cheered on every play.
>
> We grew up in the booming metropolis of Sebastian, Fl. [I get a few laughs.] Jim worked at Winn Dixie and I worked for Publix directly across the street.

We were so competitive that we would argue with my mom about where she shopped.

'Lower prices!' Jim would maintain.

'Better customer Service - Where shopping is a pleasure!' I would retaliate.

As to not play favorites, my mom would buy half of her groceries at each store.

There are so many fond memories. Many of which Jim and I reminisced on just a few weeks ago. We were both headed to Delaware for our annual Melia Family vacation. The night before, I called him and asked if he wanted to ride together.

I'll always cherish those eight hours. It was only a six-hour drive, but as many of you know, Jim was a really slow driver. During that ride, I would play this game in my head called, "Links to Jim's kids." Any time I would bring up a different subject, no matter how obscure, Jim would link it back to one of his children, especially Emily. He was so proud of all of his children. He played a CD of Emily singing over and over on that car trip.

"Perfect Pitch," he would declare confidently every time. If I would start to talk, he would turn off the CD until I was finished, so we wouldn't miss a second of Emily.

Daniel, Nick, Josh, Cecelia, and Emily, thank you for making his life so fulfilling. He always wanted a family. Thank you for making that dream come true.

> To my brothers and sisters, this tragedy only reminds me of how lucky I am to be part of this amazing family and how easy it is to forget that sometimes. I love you all. I just wish that I had told Jim that more often and I'll always wish that we were closer.

I closed by reading one of Jim's favorite stories. Although he was a big man, he had a passion for helping the little guy and always pulled for the underdog. Jim would often share this story with his students ... and anyone else who would listen.

The Starfish

> Once upon a time, there was an old man who used to go to the ocean to do his writing. He had a habit of walking on the beach every morning before he began his work. Early one morning, he was walking along the shore after a big storm had passed and found the vast beach littered with starfish as far as the eye could see, stretching in both directions.

> Off in the distance, the old man noticed a small boy approaching. As the boy walked, he paused every so often and as he grew closer, the man could see that he was occasionally bending down to pick up an object and throw it into the sea. The boy came closer still and the man called out, "Good morning! May I ask what it is that you are doing?"

> The young boy paused, looked up, and replied "Throwing starfish into the ocean. The tide has

washed them up onto the beach and they can't return to the sea by themselves," the youth replied. *"When the sun gets high, they will die, unless I throw them back into the water."*

The old man replied, "But there must be tens of thousands of starfish on this beach. I'm afraid you won't really be able to make much of a difference."

The boy bent down, picked up yet another starfish and threw it as far as he could into the ocean. Then he turned, smiled and said, "It made a difference to that one!"

-- adapted from "The Star Thrower," by Loren Eiseley

That summed up Jim. He wanted to — and he *did* — make a difference. And he did it one life at a time.

"See you on the other side, Big Guy."

I pointed to the sky and solemnly returned to the pew in the second row. I had a mixture of adrenaline and sadness.

The family quietly made our way back to the cemetery in Sebastian, and Jim's body was laid to rest next to my parents.

The week from hell was over. And so was an important era of my life.

Chapter Four

THE 162 EXPERIENCE

In Early January of 2013, I set out to complete my *162* book. I felt so close, having already written more than 500 pages. I also felt so far away as the book needed a lot of work. With Opening Day in front of us, my editor Paul and I forged ahead with that as our goal release date.

My new title and responsibilities with LegalShield in Illinois were absorbing much of my time. In addition, the freezing Chicago weather for me was unbearable. My house sat empty in North Carolina. My new girlfriend Ashley and I had broken up and I was sleeping on an air-mattress in the guest room. It was time to go home. It was time to finish my promise to my dad and complete *162*.

I called the Vice President of Sales, Tony Petrill, and we began the move to find my replacement. This was pretty simple, as Chicago native and my right-hand man locally, Mel Roberson, was the obvious choice. Within two weeks I was back in the warmer weather with a goal to publish my first book. Paul and I worked feverishly on the concept, content, and the look and feel of *162*. We asked questions like, *What is my market? Who are my readers? What kind of book do I want this to be? What kind of language? What is the message? How long should the book be?*

We plowed through deadlines and set new ones. On March 25th, we went to print. I proofed the manuscript myself seven times in four days. Cover to cover. My head was spinning, but I've never had a prouder moment. I did it. *We* did it.

Now it was time to think like a marketer. I looked again at the sign in my office that reads THINK LIKE A MARKETER.

NOTE: *As I did in my 162, from this point forward the book's point of view will shift to present tense, so the reader can experience the journey much as I lived it — as a day-to-day journaling adventure.*

Wednesday, April 3, 2013

I anxiously await as 1,000 copies of my book are delivered to my house in North Carolina. I rent a minivan and remove the back row of seats as I pile in case after case. This is my 15th annual convention in Oklahoma, but the first that I am driving to. I can already see that life as an author is going to be way more glamorous.

Just over 24 hours later, I pull into Oklahoma City, with my friends Danny Vulin and Bill Guyther. That night, I host the very first *162* book-signing/comedy show at Tapwerks, a bar in Bricktown. We rent out the entire second floor as hundreds of my friends and colleagues pile in. It is more of a variety show as some of the associates sing, rap, and recite spoken word pieces. I do one of my best 20-minute sets. My friend, comic Mark Trinidad, headlines the event. I think I was probably a little too adult for some of my audience, but they were warned!

The evening is a major success as I sell more than 500 books throughout the weekend. Stats show that 99 percent of self-published books never sell that many copies. I feel like I'm off to a good start.

One author and marketing guru that I've grown to admire is Chris Guillebeau. He wrote *The Art of Non-Conformity: Set Your Own Rules, Live the Life You Want and Change the World*. In one of his blogs he wrote that you can have a book signing anywhere, including coffee shops, living rooms, bars, etc. This would become my roadmap moving forward.

Friday, April 19, 2013

April 19th is always a special day as it commemorates the business partnership between Mike and I, as well as the anniversary of my mom's passing eight years prior. With a week's notice, I purchase 25 Yankees-Blue Jays tickets for this date. I arrange with Gretzky's, a bar close to Rodgers Stadium in Toronto, to give me an area where I can set up and sign my books.

I've learned that in marketing, a successful venture all begins with one good idea. Just one. I believe that I had one when I came up with the Rockstar Package. The Rockstar Package is $30 per person, and included is a game ticket, an autographed copy of *162*, and a pregame party at a local bar, in this case, Gretsky's. I want to give the Rockstars the *162* experience. I also want 25 people carrying *162* into the ballpark. This branding is part of the master plan. Guillebeau points out that you want an army of promoters. You must forge a relationship with them. An army of 1,000 enthusiastic promoters will carry you to the promised land, according to him.

The first night works like I thought it might. My dear friend Rob Mackenzie is my top promoter. Rob is the kind of guy that if he is excited about something, he can't help but share it with others. He bounces around from table to table, bringing and dragging people to hear about my journey. I sell a half dozen copies to the nearby patrons.

Tonight I also have my first international interview on SportsNet, which is the Canadian equivalent to ESPN. The host Jeff Sammut responded to an email that I had sent the station regarding an interview. He does the 11 p.m. – 2 a.m. slot, which includes the Blue Jays post game.

Saturday, April 20

On this day, I embark on my first "tripleheader" of the year. My tripleheader includes being the LegalShield guest speaker, attending a Yankees vs. Blue Jays game, and a stand up show to cap it off. My three favorite activities with my clothes on.

The day kicks off with a LegalShield presentation at 10 a.m. with more than 300 in attendance. This is my first time doing the new and improved presentation that was just released earlier in the week. My friends Rob and Charlene Mackenzie have set up a table and I do a book signing prior to the LegalShield meeting. My Canadian friends line up to be among the first to receive their autographed copies. I unload an entire case of 32, plus another 10 from a new case — 42 in all. There's that number again.

After the meeting, I depart for The Rogers Centre. I am staying at the actual stadium that has the Renaissance hotel attached to it. I was able to score a free room for two nights with my Marriott points.

I am an hour late for the game and do not have much of a chance to push my books. I go to Gretsky's afterward and sit next to a fanatical couple from Calgary, Alberta. I take two books out of my bag and prop them up next to me at the bar. One book infers that I am reading it, but *two* books piques someone's curiosity and begs to be asked about.

The couple next to me share that they travel all over the U.S. and Canada several times a year to attend their favorite sporting events. The wife is intrigued enough to hand over $15. I quickly eat my meal and head for Brampton.

Tonight I am working with headliner and comedy veteran Marc Trinidad. I believe in mentors and coaches. My good friend Darnell Self often says, "If someone else has already done what you want to do, why *wouldn't* you copy them? It's OK to be a copycat ... as long as you are copying the right cat."

If I was putting together a list of people who have helped me with comedy guidance and advice, Marc is near the top of the list. Not only has he arranged for me to get time at Yuk Yuks and other clubs, he is always quick to offer compliments and — just as importantly — constructive feedback.

I pull up to the Days Inn Brampton. I am a good hour early before the show starts and to my surprise the room is already packed full. Since releasing *162* the week before, I am quickly realizing that I am getting way more respect as an author.

Unlike most headliners, Marc stays in the room the entire time. Some successful comics have what I call the "too cool" attitude and only enter right before their set. Marc sits stage left with the other six comics and is as attentive as any audience member. This is the same kind of message that separates folks like Derek Jeter and Mariano Rivera from the rest. Derek will stand at the top of the dugout next to the manager, even if he isn't in the game. Many veterans will hit the locker room when they are done instead of showing their teammates that they really care.

I found out before the show that this will be a "dry" show — code for *no liquor served*. Ironically, today's date is 4/20, which is also a marijuana reference and a day of celebration for stoners. I guess one could argue that every day is a holiday for stoners. As you can imagine, this is catnip for comedians. Tonight, every comic has their own take on 4/20.

I am the forth comedian on the list tonight and learned

immediately on the significance of today's date and the irony of the "dry show."

"I was a little nervous doing a show where everybody was sober," I said as I began my set. "But it didn't take long to notice that there is not a sober person in the place!" I get a huge laugh. "I don't know how you do it. Do you have IV's attached to a bottle in your purse?

"Happy 4/20. The official holiday for stoners. Do stoners really need a day specifically for partying? Don't they do this every day? That's all stoners need is another reason to take the day off and get high.

"Stoners are a rare breed. They are way different than casual marijuana smokers. You can always tell the difference. The casual smoker is always asking annoying questions like, 'Do I look high?' 'Am I acting high?' 'Can you tell I'm high?' ... as their eyes are glued shut.

"Stoners never ask that question, mainly because they don't give a f--- what anyone thinks. I was at a party recently and I see a friend who's a 'casual marijuana smoker' walking towards me, and I ask, 'You want to go for a walk and smoke this joint?' He shakes his head and says adamantly, "There is no way that I could smoke that joint and go back into that party and interact with any of those people.

"As he scurries away, I think that's how stoners differ, cause I'm thinking, there is no way that I'm going back into that party and interact with any of those people, if I don't smoke a little bit of pot first. I wouldn't even know what to talk about."

The audience, stoned or not, are laughing. This feeling is why I do it. The endorphins flood my body. My set is rocking.

"You can tell how much of a stoner someone is by the seriousness of an event that they will attend while stoned. The more important the event, the higher they get. They'll go to a wedding stoned. Their *own* wedding. Stoners will go to grandma's open-casket funeral high as a kite and be taking selfies with the body.

"Stoners don't give a shit. They will go to court on a pending drug charge, while on probation, with two strikes, and hit the vaporizer in the bathroom.

"Another way that you can tell the difference is the terminology between the casual smokers and the stoners. Like if someone says 'puff,' that's a dead giveaway.

"You would never hear a stoner say, 'I'm going to puff that bong.' They love the bong, but they 'rip' it, 'crush' it, 'hit' it — they don't *puff* a bong.

"You ever see a stoner do a bong hit? It's a thing of beauty. They can go from zero to stoned in like 1.4 seconds. The bong hit is like the HOV lane for stoners. It's the only time they are in a hurry. They are not going anywhere; they just want to be stoned that much faster.

"You ever see a casual marijuana smoker do a bong hit? It's like watching someone give their first blowjob. You pull it out and their eyes get really big, they begin to sweat and shake a little. When they grab it, they hold it as far away from their body as possible. They have all sorts of questions, like, 'Where do I put my mouth? What is that hole in the back for? Do I stick my finger in there?'

"They never want to finish the job, either. They take forever. They are coughing, gagging, crying, telling 20-minute stories, and finally they tap out. 'I don't want to do this anymore.' Then they fall asleep."

The crowd is really into it.

"As the host said, I 'traveled' with the Yankees. Well, *with* is probably a little strong. *They* traveled. I traveled, but not exactly 'together.'"

"One of my goals is to be friends with Derek Jeter. It took me a while, but I finally got his autograph last week. Unfortunately, it was on a restraining order that he filed against me. But every relationship has its ups and downs. That is why they call it a *temporary* restraining order."

The crowd was eating it up. (I believe they call that "the munchies.") I had the crowd that night and felt great about my show.

It's great following your heart and doing what you

love. I tell myself over and over on my hour drive back how good of a set I had.

Sunday, April 21

I am meeting a friend and LegalShield associate, Dale Stoneman, at today's game. She lives quite a distance from the stadium and we agree to meet at the Rogers Centre. I promised her I'd get the tickets. Like usual, I don't have any.

It is a fairly chilly day. I'm not exactly sure of the temperature because Canadians use the Celsius scale. You can often overhear a Canadian say something like, "It is splendid today. We may even reach 12." I have absolutely no idea what that means. Although I have been taught the little equation many times, it comes in one earmuff and goes out the other.

While I may not be a temperature expert, I *am* an expert in ticket scalping. Nevertheless, I am having a hard time scoring two tickets today. There is still plenty of time as it is still 90 minutes before the first pitch.

"You looking for a ticket?" asks an approaching Blue Jays fan.

"Yes, I need two."

"I only have one available to sell. You can have it for $5

... on one condition."

Most people would walk away because they need two. Not me. I'd rather buy two singles cheaply and then sit wherever I please once inside. He explains to me that it is Edwin Encarnacion bobblehead day, and only the first 20,000 fans will get the doll. He offers me a ticket for $5, provided that I go in and then hand him my bobblehead.

This sounds like the kind of deal that I usually go for.

Even though this will leave Dale on the outside without a ticket, I bite. I hand him two toonies and a loonie and the deal goes down. Once inside, I toss back the bobblehead and the deal is complete. If only it were always this easy!

I call Dale.

"You want the good news or the bad news? I'm in for $5, but I had to go in without you."

She is still 45 minutes away, but I give her my best five minute seminar on how to effectively scalp a ticket.

162 Guy's Guide To Ticket Scalping

Rule 1. Act like you don't really care if you go in or not. Have an I-don't-give-a-shit attitude (even if you really do!).

Rule 2. Tell the seller that you just want to get in and that you have no need for a good seat. This will take their strength away. Their main selling point is always how good of a seat it is.

Rule 3. Never, ever, ever say the price first. *Ever.* Wince when the say the price. Better if you can make a face like you just sucked on a lemon.

Rule 4. Try to never deal with professional scalpers, but only fans who have extras. There's a big difference. Scalpers do this to feed their families and don't appreciate frugality.

Rule 5. Be willing to walk away. It's all about supply and demand.

Rule 6. Bracket the negotiation by counter-offering with the price that you are willing to pay exactly in the middle. In other words, lowball the offer.

Example:

Scalper: "How much do you want to spend?"

You: "I don't have a lot of money," or "I wasn't looking to spend a lot," or "I just want to get in."

Again, do not say a number and don't act excited. The scalper will either show you face value, or if they are looking to get more, will let you know that it will be hard to get a ticket today. They may something like,

"With the Yankees in town, tickets are expensive."

Let's go with Scenario One.

"Face Value is $65."

This should mean nothing to you. The information is irrelevant. The scalper certainly didn't pay face. It is all about supply and demand. Let's say your goal is to pay $25. You can't be exactly in the middle, but I would offer $10.

The Scalper will either walk away and mutter that you are a cheapskate, or counter. Let's say he says, "$40, is the best I can do. This is a $65 ticket."

The middle is now $25. Do not go there yet.

Take out a twenty. If you want to be really crafty, separate your money in advance and have only one twenty in your pocket. It's impossible to negotiate if you pull out a wad of Ben Franklins or Queen Elizabeths.

The scalper may go to $30.

Then you say, "$25 is the best I can do. Offer an explanation, if you need to. Say something like "Now I have just enough money to get home." Or "Now I have just enough to get a beer inside." This might seem silly, but if you are asking someone for a favor and you also offer a reason, no matter how inconsequential it may seem, your offer is more likely to be accepted.

I spend the next hour trying unsuccessfully to scalp a ticket inside the stadium. I am quite the sight as every few seconds, holding up one finger, I mutter, "Looking for one!" Who scalps once they are *inside* the stadium? The 162 Guy — that's who!

I am a big believer that things happen for a reason.

Exactly 30 days prior, I was at Chicago's O'Hare airport. I was on an extended layover returning from Europe. Earlier that day, I was meeting with my editor, Paul Braoudakis. One of the things that we discussed was the length of my book.

Paul was sharing with me statistics on how the longer a book is, the less likely that it will sell. At that point *162* was well over 500 pages. This is already down from about half of the rough draft I gave him in December! He wanted to get it under 300, but would settle for under 400.

With that fresh in my mind, I noticed a book as I was briskly moving through the airport terminal. I stopped in my tracks, walked into the bookstore and picked up a book entitled, *Out of My League*, written by Dirk Hayhurst. I immediately turned to the last page to discover that is was 406 pages.

The book was about a former pitcher who spent a "cup of coffee" in the bigs. For novice baseball fans, this means his trip to the big leagues was really short. I was fascinated to read the back to learn that the book was about his mostly minor league career and his journey.

His market is my market — baseball fans. I pulled a crisp twenty out of my pocket and purchased a copy. I needed to learn as much as I can about writing and marketing books. I began reading it on the flight back to Wilmington and continually laughed out loud. The best part was his style when describing his family and fellow bullpen mates. It showed me that the fans would be interested in more than just the game or score, but the characters around the game. For the last few weeks, I have been raving non-stop about Dirk and his book.

At the stadium, I notice SportsNet has a broadcast booth set up where they do the pre-game. This is a good place for me to meet the broadcasters and make some connections. I recognize former player Gregg Zaun. I stop and lean against the railing with a group of other baseball enthusiasts and noticed an obnoxious fan on my left begins to heckle the broadcaster seated next to Zaun. It is very unusual for several reasons. First off, it isn't even noon and heckling is usually fueled by alcohol. Secondly, the lanky guy in the booth is simply sitting there going over his notes and prepping for the show.

"You suck! No one even knows who you are. You were the worst!"

The obnoxious guy continues and has everyone's attention, including the tall and wily broadcaster. I am shocked that this is happening and that security isn't rushing over to bounce this idiot.

"Who are you anyway? Your career was a joke!"

The well-dressed and mild-mannered broadcaster smiles at him. This only infuriates the jerk more.

"Who did you even play for?" You sucked then and you suck now. Did you ever win a game your entire career? What was your E.R.A? You suck!"

Wow. I've never seen someone heckle an announcer. And people think Canadians are all friendly! With that, the Blue Jays pre-game commentator has had enough.

"Why don't you go get a tissue out of the bathroom and wipe your tears away?" he taunts back to the jerk fan. He starts impersonating a baby by rubbing his knuckles against his eyes while pouting. The spectators go from being uncomfortable to laughing along with him.

The heckler finally storms away. A little rattled, the broadcaster comes over to an Asian couple about 10 feet to my right to sign an autograph. They have several books that they are getting signed. He makes his way down the line and I make my way to the couple.

"Who is that?" Just as I ask, the answer hits me. I notice the cover. It is Dirk Hayhurst. Talk about Irony! I fumble through my bag and grab a *162* book.

"Hey Dirk! Can I tell you something?" He walks over. I hold up my book. "I'm an author and this is my first book. I published it last week. So I'm having a meeting with my editor …" I go on to tell him the whole story about my conversation with Paul and how I happened to see Dirk's book in the airport gift shop. He gives me his full attention as we chat on how long a book should be.

"You really went to *every* game?" Dirk asks incredulously. "I've never heard of a fan do anything like that."

"If I gave a copy would you read it?" I ask.

He agrees to read it and tweet about it if he likes it. Wow.

My job is to keep telling the story. My mission is clear: to sell a million copies. I promised my dad that I would. I fully intend on keeping that promise.

Chapter Five

GOING DOWN THE ROAD FEELING BAD

When I decide to pursue *The Last 42*, it's amazing how often that number pops up in almost everything I do. It's almost as if it's calling out to me, prodding me along, encouraging me to pursue the adventure.

When I sit down to plan out how many of my 162 books I would need over the 7-8 week journey, I make several trips to the post office and ship 10 of my boxes to New York. I can mail an entire case of 32 for $19.42. I go to Lowe's and buy a handy six-foot table for my merchandise. The total is $42.40. Additionally, my car loan number is 0142. The lot of my house is L42. Every time I look at the clock I swear it is 42 after the hour. Hmm ...

I had 30 days to get ready for *162*. I would have only 72 hours of preparations for *The Last 42*.

My doubts of a few nights ago had turned into legitimate concerns now. As I was telling people about my seven-week trek, I could hear hesitancy in my own words. I was saying things like, "if" I do it and "I'm supposed to" leave on Thursday. I know that for the commitment necessary there was no room for doubt. One ounce of doubt and you are out. Much like after Opening Day in New York in 2011, I questioned whether I was crazy or not. Oh, I'm crazy all right, but the question was *how* crazy?

Thursday, August 15

Although I am in a hurry to begin my six-week voyage, I am in a fog.

My phone is vibrating and I can see that I have already missed two calls from my sister Mary. She is crying uncontrollably. I can barely make out that her 28 year-old son Matt has hit rock bottom. Matt has had a problem with drugs and alcohol for a decade and a half. He went on a binger for days after Jim's funeral. Matt may be the closest to me of my 21 nieces and nephews and is more like the little brother that I never had.

Mary and I have one of the most honest conversations of our lives as she talks about putting Matt in a 28-day rehab. I agree that this is the best thing and that he needs help. The reality is that he has been in need of help for a very long time. Mary is hysterical and recalls an emotional and even scary last 12 hours that has Matt broken down and finally admitting his problem. Many friends have offered their empathy since, but this is a true blessing. Today is the beginning of the road to recovery for Matt. I am proud of him for taking such a big step.

I contemplate skipping my baseball trek as guilt consumes me for leaving my family in time of need. What am I going to do while he is in rehab for a month? If I don't go, I'll just sit on my couch and feel sorry for myself. We agree that I should go.

I spend the next two hours talking to a few of Matt's friends to make sure that he is being honest about everything that he is on. After a few very telling conversations, I relay to Mary that he is in need of rehab. Later that day, Matt begins five days of grueling detox. He also begins a journey that would save his life.

Something else has been weighing heavily on me over the last six weeks. On June 28th, while on vacation, I received a text from a girl that I had dated off and on since Kim and I separated several years ago.

Our relationship was volatile and many would say toxic. She is in her late twenties and we would break up and go out again as often as some change their underwear. The text was a picture of her and what appeared to be a baby bump. We hadn't seen each over the last four months and barely communicated. In essence, we were done. She had moved away from Wilmington and was living with her folks a few hours away. A trip to the doctor a few days later would confirm that bump was indeed a baby.

I had mixed emotions when hearing the news. I've always wanted children and there is a part of me that was really excited to know that I was bringing another human being into the world. I was in Delaware when I learned the news. I told two people: My sister Mary and my brother Mike.

I left vacation a day early, rented a car, and drove straight to Raleigh, North Carolina. I was relieved to learn that we were literally just two days past the legal limit from terminating the pregnancy. At least in North Carolina. But I saw the sonogram and knew that I would have to live with this decision for the rest of my life. Thank God we talked about it and that option was off the table.

For weeks, I grew more excited about the possibilities of becoming a dad. The two of us even discussed getting back together and starting a family. I knew deep down that this was a horrible idea as we drove each other crazy. We talked about shared custody. We talked about how beautiful our baby would be. My heart went out to this young lady as she had so much more to deal with than I did. She had the awesome responsibility of carrying our baby.

The month before Jim's death was one of my most difficult times. I was constantly thinking and judging if I could do it by myself. Although I have a hard enough time just taking care of me, I contemplated what life would be like as a single dad and what kind of life I would be giving my child. I read books like *Parenting for Dummies* and *First Time Dads*. I shared this information with only those closest to me.

My baby mama was living with her wealthy and controlling parents and had done a masterful job of hiding her secret for quite some time. When she finally told them, they put on the full court press. We went from open conversations to considering only one option. Adoption. Everything changed when they found out. Her parents forbid that she see a doctor in her own town at the risk of being an embarrassment to the family.

After Jim's death, I just didn't have the energy to fight about it. I gave in and agreed to give our baby up. It was the hardest decision I have ever made. I'm sure it was for her as well.

This morning I went through old photo albums and pulled out as many pictures of Jim and I as I could find.

I post a few on Facebook. In my search I also found two with Mariano Rivera. I grab these and my dad's Mass card from his funeral.

Every time I look at it, it reminds me of my final promise to him to sell a million copies of *162*.

I get in my 2007 white BMW and position the pictures on my dashboard where I can see them. I back out of my driveway with little fanfare. A little over two years ago, I had Steve Marcinowski with me and was gearing up to do something special. This time I fly solo. Just like life. You come in alone and you leave alone. A little over two years ago, I was leaving the house that was occupied by my then-separated wife Kim. This time it will remain empty.

Am I crazy? I think we have already established this. Present is the same rush of adrenaline I experienced in 2011. Gone in some way is the mystery of whether I can pull this off. Barring any major catastrophes, this should be a piece of cake. A can of corn.

About an hour into the trip I notice that I have a missed call from a 516 area code.

"Steve, it's Howie from the *NY Post*. I wanted to see if this was a good time for an interview. Call me back."

I do. He offers his condolences and we jump right in. The interview lasts a good 15 minutes. I'm back, baby! He asks all of the right questions and I feel like he has a good grasp on my mission. He tells me it will appear over the weekend.

BAM! That just happened!

I hang up, smile, and crank the music. The Grateful Dead song "Going Down The Road Feeling Bad" is on the radio. How ironic. Feeling bad for losing Jim and feeling like a badass as well. Not too many people get to live a dream even once, and now I'm doing it again.

I zip up I-95 and smile as I flash back to August of 2005 to the Anaheim Hilton (this story is also recounted in 162).

The Yankees were visiting Anaheim and were staying at the Hilton. Kim and I were living in San Diego at the time. My brother Mike and his son, Willie, were at the series with us. We purposely stayed at that hotel because we knew that's where The Yankees stayed. They lost the Saturday night game and were on a three-game losing streak.

We strolled down to the lobby bar around 11:30 p.m. to an almost-empty bar. Almost. I looked over to the left where there is a pool table. Racking the balls and asking if anyone wanted to play was the man himself, number 42, Mariano Rivera.

I immediately walked over and raised my hand like I was a third-grader asking to go to the potty, and with a cracking voice mustered up, "We'll play!"

The four of us made our introductions and Kim and I got to play first. Mo was sensational. Of all the bars that I have played in, I have never seen anyone as good. The cue ball glided down the table like his cutter. The backspin was amazing. He was partnered up with a girl who worked at the hotel Starbucks and was not very good. We won the first game because she scratched on the 8 ball.

"Yes!" I shouted with a fist pump. The Melias beat Mariano, the best closer in baseball history! We played again. Almost the exact scenario played out. But the 2-0 lead quickly vanished as Mo closed us down and won the next three.

The entire experience lasted about two hours. You always hope that when you meet someone you idolize, that they won't spoil the perception. Like he has so many times before, Mo delivered. Kind, gentle, warm, and funny, are just a few words to describe Mariano that night. We drank beer. He drank juice. Towards the end, we asked for a picture. He willingly obliged.

At one point Mike took out his cell

phone and moved towards Mo. As he was dialing, he asked the future Hall of Famer if he could leave a message for Mike's youngest daughter, Dani. She was a student at NYU's film school at the time. Mo politely said no with a smile on his face several times, but no one can escape Mike's persistency! Mo left her a message and made her day when she finally believed it was him.

Over the next few seasons, we would run into Mariano several times and he always greeted us with a warm smile and a kind word. If he didn't remember us, he sure was a good actor.

Just before midnight I roll in to my friend Jen Quigley's home in Tom's River, NJ. We say a quick hello and goodnight, as we have a big day in front of us.

Friday, August 16

We are off at 8 a.m. as we have some errands to run. Jen called me up last Sunday night and offered to accompany me to Boston. We are using her Marriott miles for a hotel in downtown Boston. This should save me at least $800. One of my goals is to go the entire trip without paying for a hotel room.

I have called ahead and the insurance office is open until 5 p.m. We roll into downtown Boston at 2:30. I write a check to the state of Massachusetts for $63 and I ask if there are any restrictions as to where I am allowed to set up my books with my newly acquired peddler's license.

The woman, who was born sometime between the Civil War and the end of WWII, goes in circles. She infers there are "some" restrictions, but she isn't exactly sure what they are. She writes down the number for the main precinct at Boston Police headquarters.

I grow more impatient by the minute as I dial the number and I'm put on hold.

My question is pretty simple. *I have just purchased a peddler's license. Where am I allowed to peddle?* I don't even really like the name. It's degrading. I get transferred around a few times. No one seems to know. I get told over and over that I am not allowed within a certain distance of Fenway. No one can tell me the exact distance. If they don't know, how can I get in trouble?

We check into the Marriott in Boston Commons. We have no tickets to game one. Child's play. When we set off for our *162* tour, I was always stressed out about having tickets in advance. After going to games every day, I realized that getting tickets is the easy part.

I go to StubHub and prepare for game 1 by using my best trick. If you go to a lot of games, like to save money, and love sitting close to the action, pay close attention.

StubHub has a feature that allows you to locate the

remaining open seats in each section. The higher the price, the less likely they are to sell at the last minute. Quite often, these expensive seats will remain unsold and thus remain empty.

These tickets are for sale two hours before the first pitch.

I check out the seats directly behind the Yankees dugout. Section 52, Row B, Seats 1-4. They are listed at $750 each. This seems nice for the first game of my tour. Keep in mind that I am not buying them, just seeing what's still open.

I do this five more times so I will have a backup plan. These tickets may make it to the scalpers and indeed get sold. I take out my newly acquired license and write down all of the seat information on the back. We head for the subway and I have my bag of a dozen books, which should cover my beer money.

The scalpers outside of Fenway are hardcore. They walk and talk fast and seem to have the entire area completely covered. They all work in unison to fix the ticket prices. They feed their families by scalping. As much as I know the game, I certainly do not want to mess with any of these guys.

As I wrote in *162*, Fenway is my favorite road park to visit. I love the intensity that the fans bring to every game. However, Boston is different. People are much

The Last 42

more patient with each other. I would say nice, but "nice" seems so trite. Sometimes things happen that cause all of us to let our guards down and just embrace each other. I personally don't hate people. I especially don't hate others because they root for a different baseball team based on where they were born. I know what it is like to scream and yell for hours for your team but to know deep down that it doesn't mean shit.

That is what I love about sports. For a few minutes or a few hours, you can find refuge in a game. No matter the sport, you can just check out of this crazy world for a while. Life is short.

We pick up a single ticket for $40. There are plenty of singles available for $100 or more. I tell the scalpers I'm not spending more than $40.

"This is Yankees/Red Sox. You ain't getting in any cheaper than $100," is the general consensus from the scalpers (in their Boston accents).

Jen is very social and is willing to talk to anyone and everyone, which often gets us in all sorts of precarious situations. We dated for a few months back in the summer of 1994. We have remained friends, but fight like Tom and Jerry.

We are wandering Yawkey Way looking for a deal. I have one finger up and am randomly announcing, "Looking for one." Jen strikes up a conversation with a vendor, the Sausage King. I only had one sausage during my record-breaking streak of 176 straight games. I am cheap and they are not good for you, especially every day.

"Steve, this guy wants to meet you," Jen announces.

She brings me over to the Sausage King booth as the first pitch nears. He has his concession stand set up 15 feet outside an entrance to Fenway. We meet and I show him a book. He doesn't seem to have much interest in reading it, but has more ambitious intentions.

"What do I have to do to get in your next book?" he asks. No foreplay, no nothing. Right to the heart of the matter.

I smile. "My main goal right now is to get into that stadium."

"How about you get me in your next book and I'll get you in tonight?" he proposes.

Hmm. Beating the system. I like the sound of this. I admire his entrepreneurial spirit. I point to the gate to make sure that I understand the terms of the deal. "You'll get me in?"

Jen is smiling big, as she knows we just scored. The Sausage King and I snap a picture of me holding his over-sized sausage (get your mind out of the gutter). I throw in an autographed copy of *162* to sweeten the

The King and I

deal. He calls his trusty partner over. He knows that Jen already has a ticket and instructs her to go in. We wait for just the right moment and he motions for me.

I follow him in as he nods to the guy taking tickets. We casually walk right past the turnstile. Wallah!

"Ok, You are on your own from here," he instructs.

Inside Fenway for free, baby. To think that I was ever intimidated to come here. Boston loves me. A great start to *The Last 42*. I can't imagine that they sneak too many Yankee fans in. Jen and I meet up and barely restrain doing a high-five. We talk a mile a minute on how amazing that was. With only a few minutes before the game starts, we make our way to the beer stand. We pick up four Blue Moons.

"Let me lead the way to our seats," I tell her. "Try to look like you know what you're doing."

We move to my first choice, Section 52, which is directly behind the Yankees dugout. The second row that I have scoped out on StubHub is still open. In Fenway, the box seats are four to a row. We sit in seats 1 and 2.

The Yankees are 7½ games out of the Wild Card and every win matters. We stand behind the Yankees and watch the first National Anthem of *The Last 42* tour. I am standing just a few feet behind the 2013 NY Yankees. Euphoria and nostalgia fill my body. I notice a Yankee that I have never seen before. I look up at the scoreboard and some guy named Reynolds is playing first base.

It is great to see Andy Pettitte taking the mound for the Yanks. He hasn't announced it, but this will probably be the last year for the 41-year-old lefty who has more postseason wins than anyone in history.

In the bottom of the first, David Ortiz (Big Papi) slaps a pitch foul into the Yankee's dugout. Mick Kelleher, the Yankees' first base coach since 2007, turns and we make eye contact. He flips me the ball. That was fast and easy. I didn't even need my glove.

We wind up making conversation with the two Red Sox fans behind me. Jen has never met a stranger. She read *162* in one sitting. To say that she loved the book would be an understatement. She most loved her shout-out, where I refer to her and her sister, Kim, as being straight out of "Jersey Shore." Our new neighbors hand over $15 and pick up a copy.

Mark Reynolds slams a homerun his first time up as a Yankee. Welcome to the family, Mark.

Jen downs her beer like a sailor on leave. By the fifth inning she is six beers in. She has been yelling for a ball the entire game. Jen means well, but is getting a little out of control. *Pace yourself*, I think to myself, *these Yankees/Sox games can go all night.*

At the beginning of the sixth, she is standing, chatting, and starting on beer number seven. Kelleher flips her a ball, but she is too oblivious to even notice. It ricochets off of her large chest. She looks up like "what was that" and then screams dropping to her knees to retrieve the rolling ball.

Mick shakes his head as if to say, "Really? You've been yelling at me the entire game!" She is ecstatic, nevertheless, and holds up her prize and celebrates like she just tossed a perfect game.

The Yankees are up 7-1. For Boston fans they are just waiting for the next time A-Rod is up so they can boo him again with everything they've got.

Jen leaves to go to the bathroom and get a few refills. Thirty minutes later she stumbles back and hands me three quarters of a beer.

"I need three books," she slurs. "I met these guys and they all want one."

I'm half pissed off, but tolerant as I am three closer to selling a million. She grabs them and off she goes. The innings roll by. My iPhone has died, so if Jen gets lost, she will have no luck texting or calling me.

Apparently she was.

These seats are so baller, I'm not going to spend my night chasing her around Fenway. I keep looking behind me as my patience is wearing thin. We stopped dating back in the summer of 1994 because of a similar situation. We were at a party and she just disappeared for hours. Déjà vu all over again. When the ninth inning begins, I decide that I'm heading straight for the exit when the Yankees win.

With Jen in front of the Green Monster

The Yanks close it out 10-3 for their fifth straight win. The recently acquired Alfonso Soriano drove in four runs, including a three-run blast in the third inning.

He reached base in all but one plate appearance and now has a Major League record-tying 18 RBIs in his past four games, going 13-for-18 with five homers. Soriano left New York in 2003 as part of the A-Rod deal with Texas. Welcome back, Sori!

As planned, I head for the exit making no effort to find my friend. I walk briskly to Kenmore Square and hit the subway. I am pissed, free hotel room or not. I make it back to the Marriott and plug in my cell phone. A minute later the "emergency texts" start rolling in. So do the voicemails. I decipher through all of the mumblings that Jen claims she was ejected from Fenway Park for soliciting. Right.

She eventually gets dropped off by her "customers" and rolls in to the hotel room and starts to state her case. She tells a tale of how Fenway security witnessed her selling books and told her that she had to go.

I don't believe her. She pleads with me. Nope. I try and communicate that this isn't a drunk fest. I am on a mission, and it doesn't include babysitting services.

"I was just trying to help you sell the books," she pleads.

"Did they see you collect money?"

"No."

"Did you collect any money?"

She is silent like it just hits her.

"Um, no. I guess I forgot with all of the excitement."

I quickly change clothes and head out to one of the nightclubs in our hotel by myself as my date passes out.

Saturday, August 17

Jen and I are barely talking. Today is the first day that I will set up a table to sell *162* on the streets of Boston. License; check. Books; check. I have no tickets, but find someone on Craigslist who is selling a bleacher ticket for $20. I am skeptical that they will even show up for $20, but we agree to meet before the 4 p.m. start.

At 11:45 a.m., I pull up outside of Fenway to the corner of Yawkey and Brookline. The streets are fairly empty since it's so early. I unload my six-foot table, *162* posters, and three cases of books. I quickly get a lot of strange looks and comments like, "You've got a lot of guts."

Seven book sales in, I am greeted by a middle-aged, slightly overweight dude who is dressed like everyone else in Boston with his Red Sox gear. I mistake his questions for interest in my book.

"What are you doing?" he asks.

I launch into the same speech I've been giving for four months. A few other people are coming up to the table and this guy doesn't look like he is a buyer. I sell a book to a young couple from New York. The Red Sox fan is still loitering by my table. He directs his next statement to Jen.

Set up and looking for trouble at Fenway

"You were the one selling these inside of the stadium last night." He then introduces himself as Head of Fenway security.

Uh oh.

I interject. "You have got to be kidding me. She was telling some guys about my book. That is called *promoting*, not selling."

"You are not allowed to sell *or* promote anything inside the park," as he forcefully points to Fenway.

"So if I tell the guy sitting next to me about a movie or a good restaurant, you would kick me out?" I challenge.

Jen is smiling as she is now relieved that I am going to believe her.

"I wasn't even doing anything and I got kicked out," she blurts.

I give her a nudge to keep quiet and to let me handle the situation, but she persists.

"I think I got kicked out because I was drunk," she admits. I shoot her a look to convey that she isn't helping.

"We asked her what she was doing and she said that she had a peddler's license, but then couldn't produce it," Mr. Security says.

"It's right here," I say as I hold it up.

He reaches over and snatches it. It is apparent he wants to shut down my operation. He begins to get on his phone.

"You can't be set up here," he says as he glares at me.

"I did everything I was told to do to comply. The state, police headquarters, and nobody can tell me the exact rules. They just keep saying that I can't set up 'too close' to Fenway."

He raises both of his hands in frustration.

"This *is* Fenway! You have your poster attached to Fenway Park."

I laugh to myself as I didn't even realize it, but that's pretty cool that I have taped both of my *162* posters to the brick wall.

"You guys are something else," I shoot back. "I am a customer and a very good one. I come here. I buy tickets, food, and beer and spend my money in your city. I've been to 176 straight games and all you care about is kicking me out."

One game into the tour and I have definitely got the Red Sox brass' attention.

He is now on his walkie-talkie that I didn't see earlier, like he is an undercover narcotics agent.

"Then tell me where I am allowed to set up," I plead.

He either doesn't know either or just simply refuses to tell me.

"Not here. You need to start packing up."

"Fine. I will pack up and move locations, I just need to know where I can set up."

He is getting tired of me. Jen continues to argue about last night.

"How can you just kick someone out with no proof of anything?" I agree with her, but am not looking to get arrested or miss today's game.

Someone walks up and asks, "Are you Steve?"

At this point, I am cautious to admit anything.

They continue, "I have your ticket."

We pull away like a drug deal and I quickly scan the date and hand my Craigslist hookup $20 for the bleacher seat. Head of security dude *really* doesn't like me now as I continue to box up my books and take down my sign.

I am pretty hopeful for book sales after my initial success and not ready to call it a day yet.

"Is across the street considered 'in Fenway?'" I ask.

He shakes his head in disbelief.

"I'm not trying to be a smart ass, I just would like a straight answer."

"I'm not telling you that you can set up anywhere. This is Fenway. You can't be here. I'm calling the Boston Police."

"Call them. They don't seem to know the laws, either. I was on the phone with them yesterday for 15 minutes and no one seemed to know."

"How about over there," I ask as I point across the street. "Is *that* Fenway?"

He just looks at me as I continue to load my 39 lb. boxes onto my dolly.

I roll over across the street, which is about 40 feet away. He just stares at me as I reset my operations. For the next hour, I hustle. He watches my every move.

I move 25 books and the cash is piling up. I'm even taking pictures with Yankee and Boston fans alike, which really seems to really infuriate Mr. Fenway.

Enter a 75-year-old man from the state of Massachusetts Licensing Dept. He is a cross between little Joe from the Benny Hill show and Barney Fife from Andy Griffith. Fenway Park security have sent in their equivalent to Mariano Rivera. All that was missing was Metallica's "Enter Sandman" as he waddles toward me. He has the tenacity of a bulldog. This guy's here to get results.

"I'm here from the Licensing Department. Let me explain that you are not allowed to be here."

I produce my license and hold it up.

"Then what good is this?"

"That is a peddler's license," he offers dismissively.

He goes onto to explain that I am never able to "peddle" before 8 p.m. He looks in all four directions of the Boston Landscape. He seems to pick the furthest building or landmark in each direction and uses that as the area that I am able to sell my books.

"Show me where it says that," I say as I hold up my license. "No one up until now cared to share with me that I was buying a worthless license. Who sells stuff after 8 p.m.?"

He turns over my license and reads it without any discovery. After a few minutes of silence, he points to a line in the smallest of possible font sizes that reads, "Must comply with local ordinances."

"'Local ordinances' prohibit you from being here," he yelps.

Part of life is figuring out what battles you are going to win and which ones you are not. Or as Kenny Rogers advises in his hit song "The Gambler," *You've got to know when to hold 'em, Know when to fold 'em, Know when to walk away, And know when to run.*

With 25 books sold, no one ejected or arrested yet, and a Kuroda vs. Lackey pitching matchup, I fold.

Just like last night, the greeting for Alex Rodriguez has been, well, not a greeting at all. And just like I did in Chicago two week earlier, I just sit and take it in. Alex and Alex alone needs to take the brunt of this.

The Red Sox starter, John Lackey, made headlines earlier in the week when he told the *Boston Globe* that he had issues with Alex Rodriguez being in the Yankees lineup while he appeals his 211-game suspension.

"I've got a problem with it, you bet I do," Lackey told the newspaper. This definitely is adding to the already-existing tension between the rivals. Lackey lets his pitching do the talking today, as A-Rod goes a quiet 0-3 with a walk.

I always try to be on my best behavior at Fenway. These fans are passionate about their Sox and their hatred for the Yankees. There is a different feel tonight, though. I call it the 9/11 effect. I was prepared for it this weekend and Jen and I had a talk that we should be extra compassionate. This city has been through a lot. Boston is a tough city. Sort of like "If you mess with one of us, you mess with all of us."

Just four short months ago, their resolve was tested. On April 15th at 2:49 p.m., the first of two bombs exploded near the finish line of the Boston Marathon.

This is the oldest existing city marathon in the world. It has been around since 1897 when it started with 18 participants. It now takes place on Patriots' Day, the third Monday in April, and this year, 26,839 had registered to run. To me, a marathon represents a huge physical commitment that pits man or woman against themselves. The ultimate competition.

This harrowing day of 2013 had a different destiny.

Two cowardly terrorists wreaked havoc on one of our country's greatest cities on one of its greatest days.

Two pressure-cooked homemade bombs went off 210 yards and 13 seconds apart on Boylston St. Three spectators were killed and an estimated 264 were injured. They were treated at 27 different hospitals. Fourteen of them had to undergo life-changing amputations.

I watched in horror and disbelief with the rest of the world. Over the next few days and weeks, the term "Boston Strong" was created to describe the amazing resolve that the city and its residents displayed.

Jen and I scalp our second ticket for $30 and use my index card system to locate good seats. My system works best when I to do it closer to the two-hour time frame. Since we left the hotel five hours before first pitch, my plans today have some holes as many of the seats that I identified have now been sold.

We begin the game in great seats, but are quickly moved as the rightful owners show up. This happens three more times. We quickly move on to the next seats on the list with little or no embarrassment.

I believe that everything happens for a reason.

We are now 20 rows behind home plate. We are seated behind a hardcore Red Sox fan who — despite their 7 ½ game lead on the Yankees — is living and dying with every pitch. It is comical as he reminds me of myself.

He is chatting with everyone around him, so it takes a while to realize, but he is at the game by himself. The 33,517 in attendance serve as his second family.

It's hard to describe the unspoken camaraderie that is apparent between the Boston fans and us. With all of the Yankees/Red Sox rivalry rhetoric, there is a feeling that there is more to life than baseball. The human spirit is alive and well in Boston.

We begin to chat up the enthusiastic fan who barely fits into his tight seat. He is not overweight, just really tall and long. When I read a book, I like to have someone to picture in my mind. If you are like me, picture Ray Liotta. I see him make the sign of the cross in addition to many other superstitions that he displays. He turns around and shares with us that he lost his mom to cancer over the last year. His eyes swell up and his attention is momentarily diverted from the game.

I reach in my bag and grab a *162* book. I ask him his name as I inscribe on the first page, "To Joey D — Live your dreams. Life is Short. Boston Strong." Those last couple of words were a nod to the unofficial city motto adapted after the Boston Marathon bombing, just four short months ago.

I quickly explain my accomplishment and the idea of the book. He is as touched as anyone I have ever gifted a book to. I watch his lips quiver and he becomes even more emotional. After quickly skimming it, he hands it back and asks if I will make an additional inscription to the memory of his mom. I do. He proceeds to hold *162* as a cherished gift. Every other pitch or so, he turns around and thanks me again. In between innings and breaks in the action, he is reading page after page. We learn that he is a public defender in Rhode Island. His wife is an executive with CVS and scores him great seats.

As the Red Sox expand their lead to 5-0, I order two Stellas from the vendor in the aisle. Joey D signals for me to put away my money. As the seventh inning begins, he jets off to get last call. He briefly comes back, places down his maximum purchase of two beers under his seat and jets away again.

When he gets back, he turns around and hands the second round back to us. That *162* book certainly went a long way. I laugh as I realize in all my games I've never seen one person go for four beers and barely miss a pitch. When you go to a lot of games these are the kind of things that you pick up on. As Yogi Berra says, "You can observe a lot by watching."

Joey D continues to chat us up and when Big Papi slams a 7th inning monstrous homerun, Joey does the sign of the cross, points to the sky, and holds up his newly-acquired *162* book as part of his ritual. I tell him about Jim and it only brings us closer together.

Joey D invites us to dinner following the game. He tells

us the story of how this is where he was during the bombings of April 15th. This is my first conversation with anyone who was in the area that day. It is interesting to watch other people listening in as well. Everyone was affected. It certainly makes baseball seem a little less important. At the same time, it is the game that brings us together.

Joey D helps me sell another six books as we sit at the bar and he picks up dinner. It probably helps that his team won today, 6-1. "Listen to what this Yankees fan did," he would share excitedly with anyone who would listen.

By the time Joey D, left for his 8:37 train, he had probably spent $200 on us.

We show up at Nick's Comedy stop just before show time. This is my first time back on stage since Jim's death, and it is surreal. One of the reasons that I love stand up comedy is that it can serve as an escape for the audience from this crazy world for a few hours.

Tonight, I'm the one who benefits as I seek refuge from my own sadness. It works as I take a deep breath and do my best to be funny. It feels good to hear people laugh.

"I think some of you might recognize me in the crowd ... well, mostly just females between the ages of 18-22, within 50 miles of Boston who aren't looking for anything serious."

This breaks the ice and gets the crowd going.

"I think that you can tell how desperate someone is on these dating sites by how wide their search parameters are: 'My ideal match would be someone within 25,000 miles, between 3'0" and 8'11", somewhere between 14 and the final stages of hospice. Ideally.

"They shouldn't even call it Internet *dating*; they should call it Internet *browsing*. That's all I do is browse hundreds of pictures. There's no dating. I saw a woman the other night who wasn't very attractive and I swiped left, accidentally poking her in the eye. I'm sorry, I thought you were my phone.

"You look at so many pictures that sometimes you see someone you recognize out in public and you're not really sure where you know them from. That's awkward.

"'Yes, I'm sorry to interrupt your dinner. Are you SweetNtasty69? I thought that was you! It's me, Boner Boy.'"

It feels good to hear people laugh.

"As the host said, I went to *every* Yankee game in 2011."

That gets met with some loud boos. I smile and hold up my *162* book.

"The name of my book is *162: The Almost Epic Journey of a Yankees Superfan*. The original title was *162: A Summer of Sex, Drugs and Rock 'n' Roll*. But that would have been very inaccurate. If I was being perfectly honest, it would be *162: The Summer of Masturbation, Heartburn, and Hemorrhoids*, which isn't as catchy."

The crowd roars. Ten minutes later I pull up to my barstool with a burst of adrenaline. I think of my big brother who never got to see me perform in a club.

Boston Strong.

Chapter Six

SEARCHING FOR DENZEL

Sunday, August 18

From time to time, I google myself to see if I have unexpectedly received any media hits. BAM! Sixteen short days after Jim's death and five short days after writing and emailing a press release, Jim and I are featured in the *NY Post*.

> **TRAVELIN' MAN**
>
> *In order to get up close and personal with the swan song of Mariano Rivera — signing autographs for fans in Anaheim earlier this season — Yankees fan Steve Melia will attend the final 42 games of Rivera's stellar career.*
>
> *Mariano Rivera likely will throw the last pitch of his Hall of Fame career on Sept. 29 in Houston, and*

> Yankees fan Steve Melia will be there, completing a 45-day journey to see the final 42 games in the career of the greatest reliever of all time.
>
> Melia, who attended every Yankees game during the 2011 season and wrote the book, "162 — The Almost Epic Journey of a Yankee Superfan," was inspired to begin another odyssey and write another book following the finish of his favorite player's Hall of Fame career, after his older brother, Jim, unexpectedly died of a heart attack on Aug. 2. Rivera was also Jim's favorite player.
>
> "When I was doing the 162 tour, [Jim] watched about every game on TV and lived 162 vicariously through me," Melia said while driving from his home in North Carolina to Boston, the first stop of his 13-series tour, which began Friday. "We had a connection through the Yankees.
>
> "To me, it sort of memorializes my brother, Jackie Robinson and Rivera. And with Mariano, I didn't want to miss it. Every game I'm not at, I feel like I'm missing something. I've sort of been looking for a reason to do it."
>
> Melia, a 43-year-old salesman who is also a comedian, said, "This is pretty simple compared to last time."
>
> There are fewer flights and far fewer rainouts and make-up games to deal with, but Melia still is going to operate on a budget which consists of cheap seats and cheaper snacks. He brings water and sandwich-

es to each game and never pays for parking, even if it means driving far out of the way.

He said his 2011 adventure was the most fun he ever has had in his life, and even if at times it was lonely, it always was worth it when he got to each stadium. To see every one of Rivera's final pitches, and feel like he is watching alongside his brother, there is no better way he could think of to spend 45 days.

"It's going to be bittersweet," Melia said. "It's like you're happy you're there, but it's going to be very sad. It's going to be very different not to have Rivera around again."

> **Yanks superfan Melia to see Rivera's final 42 games in person**
>
> MARIANO Rivera likely will throw the last pitch of his Hall of Fame career on Sunday, Sept. 29 in Houston, and Yankees fan Steve Melia
>
> **THE RUMBLE**
> AN OFF-THE-BALL LOOK AT YOUR FAVORITE SPORTS CELEBRITIES

I quickly skim the article and I'm amazed that the story has hit the wire. I see that it is online, but often stories only make the online edition. I quickly text several people in New York and tell them to run out and get a copy ... or 10.

I fold up my MacBook Air and make my way back to the room where Jen is just finishing up getting ready. She ditches her plan to blow dry her hair and joins me on the quest to hunt down the *Post*. Ten minutes later, I find a copy of The Sunday edition and smack in the middle of the sports section is a half-page article entitled, "Moments To Treasure."

I am dancing around the bodega as I announce to the small store's employees that they are in the midst of a celebrity. I show them the article and fork over $1.75 each for their last three copies.

Jen and I take a timeout to snap a few pictures of me with the *Post*. We take a quick break from our expedition to visit the Yankees host hotel. There is a line of at least a dozen fans waiting outside with baseballs and other memorabilia to be signed. This is a telltale sign that the Yankees are lodging here.

We cruise past them and enter the lobby. I quickly spot Mark, the 6' 9" head of security who is well aware of me by now. If he admires me or my fanaticism, he sure has a funny way of hiding it.

We met originally in Cleveland in 2011. We reconnected in Tampa back in May and I gifted him and Eddie, his cohort, a free copy of *162*. When we met two weeks later at the Yankees hotel lobby in San Francisco he seemed put off that I even started a conversation with him.

His reception today is a continuation of that. Instead of a smile he greets me with raised eyebrows, as if to say, "What do you want?" I open up by showing him the *NY Post* article. Third party validation is always more credible than first party.

Enjoying my 15 minutes of fame with Mark, head of Yankees security

"Hey man. Have you seen today's *Post*?" I shove it in front of his Herman Munster-like frame. Without taking his eyes off of me he grunts, "Isn't your 15 minutes almost over?"

I am thrown off by his sarcasm and have to take a second.

"Fifteen minutes? What do you mean?"

"Your 15 minutes of *fame*. Isn't it almost over?" he asks with a sarcastic smile.

I want to tell him to f--- off as I close the paper and retreat. I don't because my mother taught me better, and more importantly, he could squash me like a defenseless ant with his left pinky.

"Well, that was rude," I remark to Jen as we have a seat and I try to compose myself.

"His job is to keep the crazies away from the team. He probably thinks that you are the Head Crazy. He is just doing his job. They probably have a huge file on you," Jen says, cracking herself up.

My lackluster reception doesn't spoil my enthusiasm as I attempt to stay grounded. We decide to keep the train moving as we head for the door. In our path, and dressed sharply in a custom-tailored pinstriped suit, is Yankee bench coach Tony Pena, Jr. I nervously approach him with a 162 book and *NY Post* in hand.

"Coach, can I take a minute to show you something from today's paper?" His reception is much different as his smile lights up the room.

I fill him in on my 162 journey. His eyes never leave me as he is deeply enthralled in my story.

"Wow. This is really something!" he exclaims.

"I'd like to give you a gift of an autographed copy, if you'll accept it."

"I look forward to reading it," he offers, as I search unsuccessfully for a Sharpie. We make our way to the hostess stand and Jen walks behind and grabs me a pen.

With Yankee bench coach Tony Pena Jr.

"*Coach - 8/17/13*

Live Your Dreams. Life is Short, Enjoy the Journey
—162 guy."

I scribble my name. I hand it to him and he accepts graciously. Jen has the good sense to get a picture. I often get so excited that I forget.

We leave the hotel and still to the right there is a line of a dozen fans waiting with baseballs and other souvenirs to be signed. One of the kids must have seen me talking to Tony Pena and pops off, "Are you a Yankee?"

"No, but I *am* famous," I humbly reply.

This sparks some conversation as I pull out a copy of my book and tell my tale. A man and his son look the most interested. They are up from New York and shell over $15. Just as I am signing with my back to the entrance of the Ritz Carlton and totally oblivious, The Man himself walks behind me and gets in an awaiting Town Car. I can tell by the excitement of the autograph seekers that I just missed something big. I turn to see Mariano's smiling face sitting just a few feet away get escorted through the streets of Boston.

"You just missed Mo," Jen informs me just a little late.

I laugh that I was too busy signing an autograph to even notice the object of my new project. As we make our way down the street, I notice a very attractive female coming our way with her family. I glance over at her husband, who is holding the youngest of their two kids and realize it is Yankees outfielder and speedster Brett Gardner. I let them pass without saying a word as I turn and realize that it is tough for these guys to be on the road and stay focused, as daddy duties do not slow down.

We are switching hotels today moving closer to Fenway. We are staying at a Residence Inn that has only been open six weeks and overlooks Fenway from just two blocks away. This hotel is way out of this trip's budget and I thank Jen again for the incredible accommodations.

The bellman comes up to retrieve our luggage and Jen shares with him that we have a published author in our presence. I always feel cheap giving out a book instead of a tip, but he is enthralled with *162*. I sign and give William a complimentary copy. We talk nonstop for the next few minutes about the rivalry and what it took to attend an entire season.

By the time he unloads our stuff into a taxi, he has forked over $25 for two additional copies for his Yankee buddies. Meeting people like William are proof to me that what I'm doing is not only cool, but it is what I was meant to do.

You can tell who your real friends are by how much you are willing to share personal things with them. Jen and I must be close because I confide in her that I am having a hard time even moving around as I have developed a very painful case of hemorrhoids. After first laughing uncontrollably at my dilemma, she is more than supportive and goes online to investigate treatment options and remedies.

I debated even writing this into the story, but "my condition" is so bad that the reader deserves to know what is happening. I will try to describe it in a way to inform without grossing you out. I am squeamish myself and almost puke at Jen's advice to push them back in.

She even calls my college roommate Slug who was once married to Jen's sister and apparently once fought his own battle with the Big H. "Melia has hemorrhoids, do you have any advice for him?"

I learned that my 162 readers appreciated the realness of the story. There is nothing more real than a hemorrhoid. It makes you forget all of your other problems. So if you are reading this and have not experienced the pain and embarrassment of these ass bubbles, count yourself as lucky.

For the third straight day we make our way to my favorite road stadium without any tickets. Although Jen and I are bickering like brother and sister or a sexless husband and wife, we are having a blast.

We make our way over to the Sausage King first in hopes of scoring free tickets. We show him the Facebook post, which is a picture of he and I as he hands me an oversized sausage. I eat it mostly out of respect.

Just as I am unveiling the *NY Post* to the King, Stevie from the state Licensing Department pops up. He is following me around waiting for me to make a mistake. The King doesn't offer us a free walk-in today and we don't ask, so we move on. Jen notices a camera crew interviewing a guy on Yawkey Way. He seems very animated and we stop to watch.

After a vibrant interview, he walks away. The producer sees us watching.

"Hey guys. Did you want to say something? We are doing a special on Mariano Rivera for Baseball Tonight."

"You've got the right guy," Jen says as she pushes me forward. "Tell him what you are doing."

I show him the *NY Post* article and tell him of my quest to see Mo's last 42 games. He signals to the camera and lighting guys, "OK, let's roll!"

"I'll ask you a few questions to lead you," he says.

"I don't want to throw you any curveballs during the interview," I warn him, "but the reason that I am doing this is to memorialize my brother who passed away two weeks ago."

"OK," he offers empathetically. "Take it any direction you like."

For the next few minutes, I fight back tears and try to stay on task. I proclaim my respect for Mo, how he has been so great for the game and how much all fans — especially those of the Yankees — will miss him.

The producer tells me that it is a special that they are doing for September 16th, which is Mariano's last regular season game at Fenway and the ESPN Sunday

Night game of the week.

Jen and I are jacked and keep moving. We have gotten to know the scalpers in Boston pretty well over the weekend. It is harder to scalp with someone walking with me, though. I have Jen wait in the bar Game On, as I walk to Kenmore Square in search of our tickets. I can get them for $50 each, but am looking to score an even better deal.

I always look for singles, as they are cheaper with scalpers. They don't like having singles, as they are more likely to get stuck with them.

I grab one for $30. Then I hear, "I got one on the Green Monster." *Ding! Ding! Ding!* That's music to my ears. A minute later, I've talked the Red Sox fan down from $100 to $50.

Jen and I make our way into Fenway. Here is another trick for when you have one great seat and another somewhere else. Most people would have one person go in and establish rapport. Then come out and give the ticket to their friend. This is the oldest trick in the book. I prefer to put one ticket right over the other and hand them both to the usher.

We climb the stairs up to the Green Monster and I do just that. He looks at the top ticket and says "Let me stamp you guys, so we don't have to keep checking every time." Well played. We have standing room only, but are just as excited to look over the entire field from the historic left field wall.

As we are waiting in the beer line, Jen nudges me and points to a dynamic gentleman making his way through the crowd. Everyone is sort of lining up to shake his hand as he passes.

"You should go give him a copy of your book," she says. Neither of us know who he is, but everyone at Fenway sure does. I fight my fear instinct of awkwardly approaching a stranger and reach out my hand. He shakes it and offers me a killer smile. He introduces himself as Steve Burton and then his assistant, Storm. She is so beautiful that I am now twice as nervous.

"Hi, I'm Steve Melia. I wanted to give you a copy of my first book, 162. In 2011, I went to every Yankees game. I'm here tonight doing my next book about Mariano Rivera's last 42 games."

"Wow. That is amazing," Burton says. Some people are very good at giving you their full attention. We chat for a minute as he continues to be bombarded by Red Sox fans. We retreat back to where we were standing and I pull aside a fan and ask, "Who is that?"

"That's Steve Burton. He's the local CBS Sportscaster. His dad, Ron Burton, played for the Pats. He's the *man.*"

Jen strikes again. She is certainly great at putting us in

the way of attention-getting situations.

It's the top of the second with Boston up 2-0. I don't need the PA announcer to know who is up. The entire stadium is ringing with boos and chants such as, "Cheater!" "A-Roid," and "Nobody likes you!"

I momentarily glance down to the field as the first pitch is thrown behind A-Rod's head. The crowd cheers wildly for their pitcher, Ryan Dempster. The count moves to 3-0 with two more inside pitches. In fact, the first three pitches were not even close. The next one is a 92 mph fastball that plunks Alex in the elbow.

Alex stares down the long-haired coward. Home plate umpire and 21-year veteran Brian O'Nora rushes out and issues a warning to both benches and Dempster. Joe Girardi sprints out to vehemently voice his objection. The warning means that the next pitcher to retaliate will be tossed. Joe believes that this is unfair and that Dempster should have been sent to the showers immediately.

Instead, Girardi is the one who's thrown out.

"You can't start throwing at people," Girardi said afterwards. "Lives are changed by getting hit by pitches. Whether I agree with everything that's going on, you do not throw at people and you don't take the law into your own hands. You don't do that."

"Whether you like me or hate me, that was wrong,"

Rodriguez added. "It was unprofessional. Kind of a silly way to get somebody hurt on your team as well. Today, it kind of brought us together."

As I watch from The Green Monster, I think this is one of those times that I wish I was closer as both benches and bullpens empty. It's comical to watch the pitchers run in from the bullpens. Although they are located right next to each other, the teams run parallel until they get to the infield. If you want to fight, stay out there and fight. Don't run in to be with your gang.

Once the game reconvenes, we rejoin our conversation with Steve and Storm. The blond-haired, blue-eyed beauty already has her head buried in *162*. I pull out another copy and autograph one for her. Her smile lights up the Boston skyline. I learn that she is interning with Burton for the summer and that she is the current Ms. Maine. Gulp. My attention is now consumed with her. I've never met a Ms. Anything, and there is definitely a connection.

"Do you guys want to meet Doug Flutie? We were just about to say hi to him."

Big Gulp. Whaaaaat? Now we are talking! I guess it's true that all famous people do know each other.

For those who aren't sports fans, Doug Flutie may be best known for his Hail Mary pass on November 23, 1984 as the quarterback of Boston College. The 5'9"

The Last 42

hometown hero, connected on a 57-yard bomb to Gerard Phelan to defeat the heavily favored defending national champs, the Miami Hurricanes.

"Can you autograph a book for him?" they ask me. I pull out another from my book bag. What a difference a day makes. Friday, Jen gets kicked out. Saturday they want to kick us both out. Today we are being escorted around hanging with Boston's rich and famous.

We make our way down to the left field line. Burton says that we should wait until the third out of the inning as Flutie is sitting in the first row. I quickly inscribe, "Doug, Great throw! Live <u>Your</u> Dreams." I then scribble my John Hancock and my tagline, "162 Guy."

Steve walks me down as Jen positions herself a few rows back with her camera. Flutie stands and greets us as Burton makes the introduction.

"Doug, this is my friend and sportswriter, Steve Melia. He's in Boston writing a book about Mariano Rivera's last season."

I smile and shake his hand.

"I'd like to give you a copy of my last book, *162*," I somehow manage to squeak out.

The Red Sox fans aren't sure how to react as we cozy up for a picture. Some begin to boo and chant, "Yankees suck!"

At Flutie's suggestion, we scramble up to the vestibule to avoid any heckling. We get out to the vestibule and talk for a few minutes. I suggest that we get a photo with Storm as well.

With Flutie gone, the four of us plan out our next adventure. Burton continues to speak to someone on his cell who is locating the stars.

With Doug Flutie and Storm

"You guys want to meet Denzel?"

Oh, jeesh. You know that you are famous when you don't even have to use your last name.

We spend the rest of the night repositioning ourselves to meet the superstar actor. The Yankees, meanwhile, are down 6-3 going into the sixth inning.

A-Rod is not a big believer in revenge being best when served cold.

"Every single one of my teammates came up to me and

said, 'Hit a bomb and walk it off,'" Rodriguez said. "They were as ticked as I was."

He does just that. A-Rod connects on a tape-measure shot to center for his second homerun of his shortened season. His teammates keep it going and bat around putting up three more runs and taking the 7-6 lead.

We are inching down closer and closer to the field as Jen and I continue to drink beer and bicker more frequently. I am moving slower than normal with my hemorrhoidal situation.

For the second time in the series, she takes off and leaves the stadium before I do without saying goodbye. Unfazed, I continue to hang with my new friends as we hunt down Denzel.

With the Yankees holding a 9-6 lead, Mariano Rivera comes into the game for the first time on my tour. We are back here in a month, but you never know when it could be his last time pitching here at Fenway.

I think about Jim as I watch the oldest player in baseball take his customary trot in from the bullpen. Mo easily retires the first two before giving up a single to David Ortiz. Johnny Gomes follows with a walk to bring the tying run to the plate. Jen is missing a good game. Marino easily records the last out for his 36th save of his final season. Steve, Storm, and I race around to try and find Denzel. That never happens, but we certainly have a blast as Storm and I exchange numbers.

After the game, Alex Rodriguez commented on the eventful evening:

"I would say that today is my most emotional day as a Yankee. After I got hit by Dempster and then hit the homerun. When I look back at my 20-year career I will look back on this day and maybe the World Series days as some of the highlights of my career."

On his teammates' reaction to the plunking: "It was unbelievable. I wasn't surprised. I mean Brett Gardner, Robinson Cano, Mariano came out in his flip-flops all the way from the bullpen. That's the emotion of the game. That was a tough moment, but the homerun I thought was one of the greatest moments of my life."

A-Rod continues to grab the headlines and attention. Three down and 39 to go.

Monday, August 19

Today is one of just four days off in six weeks. Kim is in Brooklyn and my plan is to have dinner with her and the family tonight. This means that Jen and I need to get up early. I need to drop her off in South Jersey and then I need to make my way back to NYC. This would mean seven hours in the car.

There's only one problem: Roids. And I don't mean *steroids*.

My condition is much worse today. Binge drinking, sitting for hours at a time, and carrying around 40 lbs. of books certainly isn't helping. I tell Kim that I can't make it.

Jen is more than willing to drive and help out in any way possible. I can barely lower myself into the passenger seat. With only three games under my belt, I am having a hard time. I am also having a *lot* of gas and keeping it bottled up isn't helping my situation. So I keep my window down while going 70 mph. Attractive, I know. We could drive back to NJ on a tank of my gas.

I have an interview tonight with a huge Yankees fan back in Wilmington. Joe Catenacci has a local sports radio show and he has invited me on tonight. He is as jacked as anyone who has interviewed me.

"Welcome to the show. What was Fenway like? You must be having a blast!"

If only he knew. Life on the road can be a pain in the ass. Literally.

It is cool that the show is from my hometown of Wilmington. I have a few friends text me during and after the broadcast. It takes all of my energy to do the call. I try to sound as upbeat as possible.

Jen returns from the store with bags full of remedies and pain relief. She makes me tea and tries not to laugh at her old friend's condition. The only thing that has taken my mind off Jim are my hemorrhoids. A blessing in disguise? Not in a million years.

Chapter Seven

HOW'S YOUR ASS?

Tuesday, August 20

I intend to set my alarm for 7 a.m. *Intend* being the key word. At 7:45 a.m., I wake Jen up and let her know that I am running late. I have a long day in front of me as we are about to attend my first doubleheader of the year. It's a day/night, which means a 1 p.m. and 7 p.m. start.

Jen makes coffee and packs me two bags — one for snacks and one for my "condition." I am still in immense pain and don't even know if I can sit in the driver's seat for the 90-minute journey. I can't lift anything, and Jen is cool enough to drag my 50 lb. suitcase down the stairs and out to the car. I can barely walk. I forgot to charge my phone last night and barely have any juice left.

The Last 42

One of the first calls I made after deciding to do *The Last 42* tour was to head Bleacher Creature and friend Bald Vinny Milano. I tell him of my quest and he invites me to set up my books right next to him across from the *House That Ruth Built* for the remaining 20 home games! Strong!

For those of you who read *162*, you know that Vinny is the ultimate Yankees fan and knows everyone in or around the stadium. He is very generous to open up the sidewalk outside of Billy's Sports Bar, which is the daily meeting spot before and after the game for the Bleacher Creatures and other hardcore fans.

Also, as one of only a handful of people to complete the rigorous 162 trek as a fan, he wrote the *162* foreword. That certainly should help book sales on River Avenue.

Thirty minutes into the trip on the Garden State Parkway, my dashboard beeps and I look down at the gas gauge, which is showing half full. A thermometer appears. Ten seconds later it flashes, turns red, and my 2007 BMW will no longer accelerate. I click on my blinker and flasher and make my way over two lanes to the side.

I pull over on a very narrow raised pavement area and for the first time in two years, I come to the realization that I am going to miss a game. I own the world record of 176 in a row and now I can't even do four. Cars are zipping past me at 80 mph.

All of my years of reading self-help books is paying off as I calmly sit and contemplate my options. Kim has been telling me for months to renew my AAA membership. I did not. The consequences of missing a game and standing up Bald Vinny overtakes me.

I wait 60 seconds. I decide to cut the engine, knowing full well I might not get it restarted. I look at my watch. Just after 9 a.m. My GPS shows Yankee Stadium as an hour and five minutes away. I push the BMW ignition button and she starts right up. I wait for an opening to clear and slowly gun it.

This works for 20 minutes until it happens again. The exact scenario plays out as I sit on the side of The NJ Turnpike. Sweat drips from my face as I try to survey my situation.

The phone rings and I see it's Kim.

"I can't talk, I'm in the car," I convey on speakerphone. I tell her my engine trouble and update her on my "caboose" trouble. She laughs and wishes me luck.

I drive off again and hope to keep driving in the right direction and get as close as I can to NYC. I should be more worried about crossing the George Washington Bridge. I think of my brother Jim and ask him out loud, "How about a little help, Big Guy."

As usual, the traffic across the GW is bumper to bumper. A car is broken down in the right lane with smoke pouring out of it. I am praying that I'm not in the same boat in a few minutes. I quietly whisper affirmations: *You can do it. Just a few more miles. That's the way. Keep it going.*

Fifteen minutes later, I am back on the side of the road. I'm starting to get the hang of this, though, as I wait patiently for two minutes and take off again. I know almost nothing about cars and hope that I'm not causing permanent damage.

Just after 11 a.m., I pull in front of Bald Vinny's House of Tees On River Ave. Vinny sees me and begins to look around for where I might set up. It takes every ounce of energy to lift my six-foot table, and three cases of books individually and carry them the 30 yards. I'm trying to look cool, but it's hard.

I recognize Vinny's main guy, George, who sells Vinny's shirts at every game. I introduce myself. He points out where I should set up and I pile everything in my space.

"I'll be back," I announce as I slowly and deliberately ease back into the driver's seat. I stroll down River Ave. and look to extend my streak of *free* parking. In more than 80 home games, plus the playoffs and rainouts, I never paid for parking in Da Bronx. The 162 Guy doesn't pay for parking ... umm, usually.

It would be so much easier if I could just pull into a

lot and pay $20. I consider it as I drive around to no avail. Maybe a lot of people read my book and now have the same idea. I drive past the stadium on my left and hope for a miracle. I can barely walk, and the idea of one of my mile specials isn't very appetizing.

After two rights, I am on the Grand Concourse. This is where I parked 80 percent of the time. Nothing. I take a right on Walton and ... BAM! There is my spot.

I check the times. No parking 8-9:30 a.m. Tuesdays and Thursdays. I'm in good shape. Only a mile walk.

I lock it up and limp to my new pre-game destination. Being a fanatic is a young man's game. The Bleacher Creatures begin to roll in one by one. I am immediately embraced as one of the regulars. Udi comes over and buys a book.

"How have you been, man?" he asks cordially. We got to know each other well as he is never far from Vinny in the bleachers.

As I am talking to my first potential customer, the train rolls by overhead and we temporarily stop our conversation. This happens about every four minutes.

A few times I try to yell over the train, but I quickly learn to conserve my energy and simply remain quiet and wait out the noise. Sort of makes it hard to sell.

I move 13 books before the game, mostly to The Crea-

George, Udi, and me

tures. A few days ago, I posted on Facebook that I was looking for tickets to games. In exchange I would sit with that person, answer their questions, and tell them jokes. I had one taker. His name is Junior. We met through Facebook a month prior and today he is like my guardian angel. He read *162* and is eager to be part of *The Last 42* journey.

He shows up just after 11 a.m. bearing gifts. First he unveils a "shadowbox" entitled *The Last 42*. He gives it to me as a welcome present. All the other Creatures start to come over to my table and admire his work. I am starving as I didn't have time to eat in between breakdowns.

I'm not sure if Junior read my mind or heard my stomach growl, but he kindly offers, "Can I get you something to eat?" Normally I am way too polite to accept such generosity. But since I am stuck in front of my booth, I eagerly accept.

"Man, I would love a tuna on rye from the Court Deli," I tell him.

My new friend zips away. He returns quickly with my nourishment and also hands me two tickets. One for each game.

"Here's a ticket for tonight's game," he says. "I can't go."

Oh, Junior, where were you in 2011? You rock! I look at it and start to hand one ticket back, as I noticed it was for tomorrow, not tonight.

"Keep it. I can't go anyway," he replies.

Junior has scored us some nice tickets for game one. Section 119A. He is also an enthusiastic promoter of 162 as he solicits anyone and everyone within earshot.

"Meet the guy who went to every game. All 162. Can you believe that?"

My next dilemma is what to do with all the inventory during the actual game. George volunteers to keep an eye on the merch. He will spend from 10 a.m. through the end of the second game on River Ave. hawking t-shirts. George and Bald Vinny certainly know how to hustle. After just one pre-game it is impressive to watch them in non-stop action. I've been in sales for 20-plus years and I'm learning some new sales tricks. Welcome to The Street ... or better known as The Avenue.

It was definitely way easier just going to the games. Not as easy lugging, hawking, and packing all this stuff, day after day. I autograph a book for George. I am having a hard time reading this guy. On the outside he seems like a typical New Yorker. Sarcasm is his second language. I learn that deep down he is a big teddy bear.

Junior was a great help when I was hurting the most!

Junior and I walk over together. He is walking way faster than me. I'm walking like my grandmother. He is continually turning around, waiting for me to speed up. Just as I enter Yankee stadium, he offers to buy me a beer.

"I'm good," I say as I laugh to myself that I

have just turned down a $12 beer. Definitely a first.

I pull him aside. "Junior, I know we just met, but there is something I need to tell you." His eyes get wide with curiosity. "The reason I'm walking so slow is that I have a horrible case of hemorrhoids," I whisper. Without missing a beat, he consoles me and admits that he has had them in the past as well. I tell him that I'm not sure how long that I can sit. Junior graciously lets me sit in the aisle seat.

My first game at The Stadium in 2013 has a few cool milestones. Down 4-0, Robinson Cano connects for a three-run shot and his 200th career homerun. Chris Stewart, who hasn't gone yard in three months, puts the Yankees on top 6-4 with another three-run blast. Ichiro Suzuki collects two hits, putting him at a combined 3,999 (between his stats in the U.S. and Japan).

With the game in the bag, I leave my seat to return to book sales. Joba Chamberlain comes in to pitch the ninth. Jose Reyes hits a soft grounder back to Joba as the pitcher slips and clumsily lunges at the speedster. The two collide and Joba is a little shaken up. The game is temporarily delayed as I try to decide whether to stay or go. I wait at an exit to make sure I do not miss anything. Girardi leaves him in and that's my cue. By the time I get to my book table on River Ave., I learn that I missed Mariano coming in for the final two outs.

I have to get better at gauging my departure. I am supposed to be here to watch Mariano and I miss him pitch the final two outs?

In addition to my pain, I am exhausted. I close up shop at 6:45 and head over to scalp a ticket. I usually start at the corner of River and 161st. I hold up one finger.

I turn down offers for $40 and $30. I make my way to the ticket office. This is another one of my tricks. I get in a long line for tickets and occasionally a generous fan will walk by and just hand you a comp. I don't have the patience today to wait and keep moving.

I hear a conversation with two businessmen negotiating with a buyer. I listen intently and finally interject, "What do you guys have?" For some reason the guys give up and hand us both a Delta Suite ticket. I grab a *162* book out of my bag and autograph one for the generous season ticket holder. I've never had the good fortune of sitting in the suites, but this is just what the doctor ordered. I point up at the sky and thank Jim.

The seats are all padded as I get up every inning and take a walk. In the fourth inning, a foul ball is ripped my way and I put my hand up to protect myself. The ball bounces off my left hand and stings so badly that I momentarily forget about my hemorrhoids. I need a new glove. I silently curse the unknown thief who stole mine in Oakland when I set my glove and a *162* book down and inadvertently walked away. Upon my return 10 minutes later, the book was there, but no glove.

I guess the thief wasn't a big reader.

Jason Nix delivers in the seventh inning with a solo shot to tie the game.

By the ninth I have resigned to standing. If there is ever a game that I wanted to leave, it's this one. But I'm glad I didn't. As I hobble back from the bathroom in between the eighth and ninth inning, I hear Metallica's "Enter Sandman" and the crowd beginning to cheer wildly. Wow, three games in a row. With our playoff chances dwindling, every game counts. Rivera gives up two hits, but strands the runners.

Bottom of the ninth. Jason Nix is up with Ichiro pinch running at third. Nix rips a base hit to left and Ichiro scores. Walk off, baby! Sweep! Mo (4-2) grabs the win as the Yankees are 4-1 on *The Last 42* tour and 8 of 10 overall. This helps ease the pain ... a little.

I give fist bumps to George and Vinny as I arrive on River Ave. I quickly assess my situation. I am so beat. I pull Vinny aside, "Hey man, can I talk to you?"

He raises his eyebrows.

"Look I know that we are just getting to know each other and this is really embarrassing ..."

I can only imagine what is going on in his head.

"I've got a really bad case of hemorrhoids. Is there any

way that you could just take my stuff with you in the van?"

He laughs. "Wow my ass hurts from sitting through *two* games. You must be *really* struggling."

My superfan hero agrees and tells me to go home. I am eternally grateful as I slowly and delicately begin my one-mile walk. I should have asked him for a ride to my car. I'm not sure if I should laugh or cry following my first day in Da Bronx. One small step for me — one giant leap for those with hemorrhoids everywhere.

I get to my BMW and turn on the radio. I smile as I hear Grateful Dead's "Uncle John's Band." This is one of my favorite songs. In 1976, my brother Mike opened Rising Tide Natural Foods on Long Island after hearing a line of this song while deciding what to name his new store.

I laugh as I hear the first line, which sums up my day.

> "Well the first days are the hardest days, don't you worry any more,
>
> cause when life looks like Easy Street, there is danger at your door."

My smile fades away as my car breaks down for the fourth time of the day. I am now on the narrow shoulder of the Cross Island Expressway. *Please just let me make it to my brother's house in Rockville Centre.* I negotiate with God as I whisper a quick plea for help. I repeat what I did earlier and within minutes I am back up to 70 mph.

Just as I get on the Southern State Parkway, my warning beep chimes, the temperature gauge appears, and I am on the side of the road again. I put my flashers on and wait for three minutes. It starts up and 10 minutes later, and 16 hours after I left South Jersey, I pull into my temporary quarters.

I gingerly enter my new pad and I am pleasantly surprised to see a plate on the stove with tonight's dinner and a welcome note from my sister-in-law Maureen.

> *Welcome to your new home for the next six weeks. Great sweep today. Dinner is on the stove. Your room is the first one on the right upstairs! See you in the a.m."*

Whew. I made it.

Wednesday, August 21

I feel like a new employee at my first week on the new job. I want to get there before Vinny, so they don't have to go through the trouble of unloading all of my stuff.

Maureen arranged for me to drop off my car with their mechanic. They are kind enough to lend me their truck for tonight's game as my BMW gets the day off.

Vinny pulls up the van as I wait with my Court Deli sandwich. Without missing a beat, he yells across River Ave., "How's your ass?"

"Better than yesterday," I yell back "but I'm not out of the woods yet."

I sell only one book before the game to a woman named Melody. She is in a wheelchair and hasn't missed a home game in the new stadium. That is 81 games a year since 2009. That is 324 with 63 home games so far this year. That's 397 and counting. Incredible. She is as tough as any New Yorker, but has an amazing demeanor. She's actually one of the sweetest people I've ever met. I am meeting lots of folks like Melody who never — and I mean *never* — miss a home game.

And tonight is another great one.

Ichiro connects in the first inning off knuckleballer R.A. Dickey for his 4,000th professional hit (between Japan and MLB) with a line drive single. The Yankees empty the dugout like they had just won the pennant and mob the future Hall of Famer, who bows to acknowledge a standing ovation from the crowd.

Suzuki's 2,722nd hit in MLB also moved past Lou Gehrig on the all-time hit list.

Alfonso Soriano has cooled off since Friday night in Boston with a weak 0-17 slump. He snaps out tonight with a monster shot to left in the 8th to break a 2-2 tie. From my angle in the bleachers, I can see Mariano Rivera warming up in the bullpen. It's Mo time. He comes in for the fourth straight game to earn his 37th save.

I arrive home to dinner on the stove again. Someone wants to be in the next book!

Thursday, August 22

Maureen drops me off at the mechanic. Apparently it isn't cheap to replace a water pump in a BMW. $1,670 to be exact. That should pretty much eat up any profit from selling books for the next 36 games that I was hoping for. The mechanic hands me the bill that notates only the total. There's no itemized breakdown or anything.

"Seems expensive. I guess you guys aren't Yankee fans," I say sarcastically as I surrender my Visa to the greasy-handed owner.

"That *is* the Yankee fan discount. The parts in these things are hard to get to." He continues to talk in automobile lingo as I tune out and watch the light rain come down.

Tired, broke, wet, and in pain, I cautiously lower myself into my car.

"Yankee Stadium," I dictate to my GPS. It would be funny if my GPS could talk back to me.

What do you have to mope about? You are going to a Yankee game today. You are a published author and wrote a book about the Yankees. You know how many people would trade places with you? Life is short. Enjoy the Journey.

Sometimes we just need a pep talk, or at least a reminder, even if it comes from our GPS.

The rain continues and I hope I will get to sit out my "book signing." I dial George as I get closer to NYC to ask for a weather report. He tells me it drizzled a little before, but it's nice now. Not what I was hoping for. So much for getting a break.

At 11 a.m., I drop off a case of books, my six-foot table, and my posters.

For the third straight day, I find free parking and walk past all of the paid parking lots.

"I oughta kick your ass," says the 6' 5" mountain, George. I hope he is kidding, but it gets better. "You had me crying on the subway last night. That letter to your dad. That was really powerful. Here I am on the subway last night reading your book with tears rolling down my cheeks. I finished your book in two sittings. It is a great story. Way better than I expected. It was about so much more than baseball."

Built like a Jets offensive lineman, I'm guessing that George doesn't cry that much. This is one of the things that I love about being a writer. I can help someone experience emotions that otherwise they may not.

"Thanks, man." I am truly touched and reminded again that I have a story to tell to about 998,000 more people. It is almost indescribable the feeling that I get when someone reads my book. I put so much time and effort into telling the story. Having someone dive in, read it, and then like it, makes it all worth it.

"I am really sorry to hear about your brother," offers a vibrant and attractive young lady who I have never met before.

"Thank you for saying that. I'm Steve Melia."

I know how difficult it can be to offer condolences, especially if you didn't know the person. Many people do not know what to say and I get that. She is kind enough to offer her sympathy and she has never even met me.

"My name is Becki. I read *The Post* article. It is pretty cool what you are doing."

I am blown away by her kindness. My sunglasses conceal my teary eyes.

At 12:45, I pack up and thank George for watching my stuff. I enter the stadium only to realize that the tarp is still on the field. This game is not starting on time. Entering the stadium before checking is a rookie mistake.

I am working on a new streak. I haven't had one beer at all three home games so far. I am going for four straight. I'm no doctor, but I'm guessing alcohol doesn't help my hemorrhoid situation. I can barely walk and have a harder time just sitting, so I just lean against a wall. I see Bald Vinny. He doesn't usually make his way out of the bleachers to the rest of the stadium.

"You stuck in here too?" he asks.

"Yeah. What about getting out through the Hard Rock? There is a smoking section there."

"I've had a few run-ins with the security supervisor. She has it out for me. What she doesn't get is that I run a business and a lot of times I have to leave to attend to things. I went over her head once or twice and now she has it out for me."

The Superfan Bald Vinny pays for his own tickets and apparently doesn't get many breaks. Our conversation is suspended several times by fans who recognize us and want photos and autographs. OK, full disclosure: *Bald Vinny* is asked to be in the picture ... I am asked to be the *photographer*.

He is a great ambassador for Yankee fans and always takes the time to talk, snap a picture, shake a hand, or autograph something and never rushes anyone along.

It is funny to watch how crazy fans are to meet him. What people do not see is how hard he and George work every day.

I'm not sure if I look disappointed or Vinny has just been watching closely, but he asks in an empathetic way. " Selling your books isn't as easy as you thought, huh?" I shrug. "I think that on the road you are more of a novelty item. People just want a souvenir." He points in the direction of River Ave. "Here, you are just one of the crowd trying to hustle."

I probably would have packed in it sooner, but his observation takes a turn towards a motivational speech.

"It will pick up," he says confidently. "The Baltimore series next week will be huge and then we have the Red Sox coming to town. Things will get better."

It might not seem like much, but this is all I need to put a little gas in my tank. After walking around the stadium and being totally bored I make my way to the Hard Rock Cafe. I give in and order a $9 Yuengling. I sip it slowly.

For the next two hours, there is no sign of a game. This is like being locked in a different kind of prison. Instead of being raped by inmates, you get raped by beer and food prices. The word at the bar is that they are going to get this game in as it's Toronto's last visit to New York this year. To generate some *162* sales, I put two copies on the bar. A nicely dressed couple next to me takes the bait.

"What's with the books?" they ask. Not only do they buy a book, they buy my second beer. Now we are talking. I'm back!

At 4 p.m. we get word that the game will start in 30 minutes. The couple ask me where I am sitting and I share with them that I have an upper decker, but I like to move around. They tell me they have an extra ticket (in the first row of 114A) and that I am welcome to join them. They are extremely pleasant and it is nice to have company, so I gratefully accept. We are treated to a great game as the weather breaks and it turns into a gorgeous summer day.

The Yankees will often run special promotions on days like this in which the fans have been inconvenienced. Because the game started 3 ½ hours late, today is one of those days. An announcement is made that anyone with a ticket for today (used or not) can trade it in for a free ticket to another game.

After sensing my excitement and need to stay on budget, my new friends confess that they won't be coming back again this year and offer me their ticket stubs, *plus* their extra ticket. I walk out of there with five free tickets to upcoming games.

In other news, Becki and I become Facebook friends.

Very well played, sir!

Chapter Eight

PERFECT PITCH

Friday, August 23

This is my first of seven flights for the tour. I have arranged to stay with a couple that lives a few towns over. I'm sitting in JFK Airport's Terminal 4 with a bagel and a steaming hot cup of coffee. Three weeks ago today we lost Big Jim. I still can't believe it and my mood changes instantly as I remind myself of our loss.

For the first week it was the very first thought I had in the morning. *My brother Jim is dead.* Now I am making it a little longer without thinking about it first thing in the morning. I feel guilty for adjusting so quickly. I have allowed myself to get engulfed in Yankees baseball. In some ways it is good to have a distraction, in others I feel bad for having fun.

My mind wanders back to North Carolina. The baby is healthy and we found out yesterday that we have a girl on the way. I am having a hard time sleeping as my ex-girlfriend is now a full six months pregnant. I know that I am doing the right thing, but I just feel so helpless. I still haven't signed the adoption papers and made anything final, but I did give my word. Guilt overwhelms me for not doing more and raising my daughter.

I think of my nephew, Matt, who has been in rehab for seven days. I send him positive energy in the form of a quiet prayer. It's the only way to get rid of that feeling of helplessness that can overwhelm me. Matt is getting the help he needs and while thinking of him going through a grueling detox doesn't put a smile on my face, I know that he has begun the brave journey to take control of his life.

Jim would be jacked at what's going on. Some may even believe that he has as much to do with our winning streak from above as anyone. Either way, he would want me to have a great time as I memorialize him. I've made sure to spend a quiet moment at each game in thought.

Tonight, Jim's wife Machelle and the five kids are loading up and heading west to meet me in St. Petersburg. I can't even imagine the loss their family is experiencing. Jim stayed single until he was 38. Some people are unsure whether they want to have families. Jim was always sure he did. They married after a few years of dating.

My late Uncle Tom, who lived next door to us for Jim's first 12 years, summed it up best. "We knew Jim was lazy, but come on!" Jim adapted well to his new role as a dad. With five children heavily involved in theater and sports, Jim spent as much time as a chauffeur than he did as a dean. It was obvious to me — and anyone who spent time with him — that Jim loved and embraced his role as a dad.

Our family has been going on summer vacation together for 29 years. A month prior to Jim's death, he and I drove from Wilmington, NC, to our vacation destination of Bethany, Delaware.

Originally, we weren't going to drive together, because Jim wanted to leave a day early. I remember calling him the night before and suggesting that I get a ride with him. Thank God I did. On the eight-hour journey, we recounted old memories and shared new ones.

As any good parent, Jim would never admit that he had a favorite. With that being said, he spoke nonstop of his youngest, Emily. Emily is now 14, with blond hair and blue eyes, and has the voice of a seasoned Broadway star.

"You have to listen to this," I recall Jim imploring as he

hit *Play* on his CD player and Emily's voice boomed in surround sound.

"That is what you call perfect pitch," he boasted proudly.

He was right. It was hard to believe that we were listening to a 14-year-old singing "Phantom of the Opera."

Emily's talent is matched by her modesty and only recorded herself so Big Jim could listen in the car. Proud does not do justice to how Jim felt about Emily or her siblings.

Later that night, I watched Jim deal firsthand with a sticky situation that involved Nick and the local police back in Florida. He remained calm as authorities at a party called and reported that the family car was left parked at a party that had been broken up by the police. These situations were not rare in our family as any family with seven children can relate. Jim waited to hear from Nick and get his side of the story. Like Jim, Nick is attending FSU, and they resolved the situation calmly and fairly.

"I think it's a good thing that he felt he shouldn't be driving," Jim said. "Nick is a good kid. He sure isn't doing anything that we didn't do."

Machelle and the family arrive in style. There are seven in the party, which also includes Daniel's girlfriend. By arriving "in style" I mean they are all wearing Rivera shirts. The sight makes me smile. Talk about doing *The Last 42* right.

This should be called Melia Family night as my sister Eileen and her husband Michael made the drive over as well. The McElwees moved to Florida just after I graduated from high school to be closer to my parents. Eileen may be the hardest hit as she and Jim both were in education in the same district. She is confronted daily with the death of her "little" brother.

Our meeting spot is Ferg's Sports bar directly across from Tropicana field, better known as "The Trop" to locals. For years I have hung out at this bar and watched it expand every year. In May, I picked up the phone and asked Mark Ferguson, the owner, if I could use Ferg's for my Rock Star package. Although I spent more hours in that bar than I have in a library or church in the last 10 years, I'd never met Ferg. Without batting an eye, he agreed and even offered to get me on the radio show that they do live from his upstairs bar.

Of all the bars in all of the baseball stadiums, Ferg's is my favorite. Friendly staff, reasonable prices, and an accommodating owner are a few of the reasons. Ferg supplies a table for me to set up a table and promote 162 for all three games.

On 98.7 FM, I make some pretty big predictions about the series. Yankees starter Hideki Kuroda can't back up my big promises in game one as he gives up four homeruns. Yanks lose 7-3 and my record moves to a still impressive 6-2.

This night was special, though, for reasons bigger than baseball. Two families came together to celebrate the life of a man who made a difference. Before the game, I presented the first foul ball from Fenway to the family, handing it to the youngest son, Josh. I also give them a copy of the *NY Post* article. They read it enthusiastically and one by one passed it along.

As the game got out of hand, Machelle shared with us that Jim was really more of a Mets fan when they met a decade ago. Part of the relationship agreement was that his allegiance would be only to the Yankees. In fact his email was My8yankees.

I'm sure that Jim was looking down on us with a big smile. I was confident that his spirit was going to produce a comeback victory. Either it doesn't work like that or maybe Jim was trying to teach us a bigger lesson tonight. There is more to life than winning and losing.

Maybe he is saving his magic for the pennant run.

Saturday, August 24

I wake Saturday morning to the realization that I have a *lot* of extra tickets to today's game. Today is our first *Last 42* Rockstar package. As with *162*, my Rockstar customers today receive a book, a ticket, and a pregame celebration at Ferg's Sports Bar.

Rather than getting my normal 25 or so, I bought 42 tickets, thinking that would be more appropriate. I have 20 sold. Oops. I post on Facebook that I have extras and text a few friends who still haven't responded. I notice on Craigslist that a mom and her little boy want two tickets and have no money. They have a picture of them holding hands on the beach and they are both pretty cute. I text her that it is her lucky day and she can pick up two tickets at Ferg's.

Friends and LegalShield associates, Keith and Amelia

Wann, say they'll take two and that would put us at 24. Still 18 to go. Keith is the one who got me on the field back in May. They are moving this weekend, but don't want to miss the fun.

It is 10:45 a.m. and I jump on StubHub and list 16 of my tickets. I list them for $32.50 each. With fees, I will break even. This takes a while, as you must enter in the barcodes for each ticket.

At noon, I have a conference call scheduled with Kim and Mike. Kim is still living in San Diego and is currently serving in her role on the Executive Advisory Board. As always, she has a list of topics and we talk about how we can all work the most effectively with me on the road for another five-plus weeks.

At 4 p.m., I arrive at Ferg's for day two. I'm a little stressed about having all of these tickets. I take my 15 extra tickets to the front of Ferg's where the scalpers hang out. One guy in particular is there whom I have recognized for years.

"I have 15. You want them?"

"Sure," he says without hesitation.

Scalpers are pretty crafty and I am a little leery when he responds so quickly. I tell him face is $19. For once, I follow my own advice and ask him how much he's looking to spend without quoting a price.

"I'll give you face," he says. He whips out a hundred, two fifties, and five twenties and we have a deal. I actually make $15. Ha.

I almost skip back to the book table as the weight of the world is slightly lifted. I thought I was going to be out hundreds, but now I'm in great shape.

Ferg's is packed with Rays and Yankees fans alike getting a chance to say goodbye to Mariano Rivera and take in a game with playoff implications. I go upstairs for a quick radio interview with 98.7. This is the fourth time they have had me on the air and they are treating me like an expert. We talk about the excellent Rays pitching and the illustrious career of Rivera.

The Rockstar party has multiplied as the sun is shining and temperatures are in the high 80s. The party begins as Jim's friends continue to roll in.

Ray Ahrens is a former student of Jim's I met over Facebook last month. He tells me how he looked up to Jim, even though Ray comes in at 6' 9". Like Jim, Ray seems to be a gentle giant.

Without any prompting, he immediately starts sharing stories about Jim.

"I get asked a minimum of twice a day if I ever played basketball," he says. "That answer would be no ... if it weren't for Jim Melia.

"I had tried out to the basketball team in the seventh grade and did not make it. I sprouted six inches over that summer. The first day of school the next year, I remember seeing your brother come walking across the courtyard headed right for me. He literally grabbed me and said, 'Let's talk. You are playing basketball.'

"Honestly, I didn't like the other coach at all and would have quit many times, but I liked being around Jim so much and didn't want to disappoint him. So every day when I get asked that question, I think about Jim."

Very cool. There is nothing more rewarding than some-

Signing books at one of my favorite bars, Ferg's

one going out of his or her way to offer a compliment to someone who isn't even around to accept it. Ray drove across the state to spend a few hours with us. He doesn't even really like baseball, but felt he had to be here today.

Jim's former high school classmate and long time friend, Georgia, is in the house as well. Within hours of Jim's death she proposed and organized The Jim Melia Foundation. The Foundation offers complimentary after-school tutoring services as well as help with financial aid, SAT prep, and other important tools to prepare students.

Jim and Georgia were really tight in high school and had stayed friends. Georgia is a mother of four and lost her husband 10 years prior to a heart attack. She and one of her sons drove over with Jim's lifelong friend, John Frazier. In addition to spearheading the foundation, she is organizing the first annual Jim Melia Foundation Golf Tournament.

I am making the rounds as friends from the past and Yankee fans from social media are arriving to pay their respects. At 5 p.m., my iPhone, which had been charging behind the bar, chimes and I check my texts and email. I quickly notice an email from StubHub reading, "SOLD."

Uh oh.

It totally slipped my mind! I scroll down and my heart beats faster. Another StubHub email. And another. And another. Holy shit! One minute I'm soaking in the beautiful Florida sunshine, the next moment I'm freaking out. Two fans walk up to the table.

"What have you got here?"

I do my best to remain calm and tell the *162* story. They buy a copy each and I nervously scribble an inscription along with and my calling card, "162 Guy."

I maneuver my way through the very packed Ferg's. I squeeze my way through and spot my scalper. I wait until he is done with a customer while eyeing his tickets. I waste no time.

"I f----ed up. Some of the tickets might not be good. I listed them on StubHub and forgot all about them."

His look of anger is unmistakable as he begins to separate mine from the rest of the group. I apologize profusely as I frantically scan my phone to identify which ones are left. He has 10 of the 15 still.

I begin to name the seat numbers that already sold and do my best to cross reference. After I apologize for the third time, he interjects.

"It's not about being sorry. This is my reputation. Plus, I offer double your money back on bad tickets."

Perfect Pitch

"Well, like I said, I'm sorry and I'll do whatever I need to pay for my mistake," I sheepishly offer.

I make my way back to the backyard area and notice four people who bought my package whom I have never met before are waiting at my table.

"You must be the 162 guy," one of them says.

"Hi. Sorry if I look frazzled." I explain that I may have oversold the tickets. "These should be good though," as I hand over two tickets with two copies of *162*.

A guy about my age, who has his 6-year-old son with him, raises his eyebrows and gives me a look of concern. I call my brother Mike over.

"I've got a real situation here. I need your help." He knows me well enough to know when I am in over my head. I tell him my dilemma and hand him my phone. He quickly begins jotting down the tickets that have sold on StubHub.

I lay out all the remaining tickets. With many of the Rockstars watching, we are so focused that we must look like we are trying to land Apollo 13. Houston, we have a problem!

I squeeze back out to the scalper who stands on Central Avenue. He's not happy to see me as we go over which tickets were sold online. He has sold five and returns the other 10. I hand him back $200 and we agree to assess the damage later.

The Rockstar group continues to grow as my cousins Trish and Kevin Mahoney arrive with their daughter Shannon and her husband Andrew. Trish's mom and our dad were sister and brother and the cousins did everything together growing up.

Shannon is an elementary school teacher and has a student named Mariano Alex Rodriguez. Talk about being a fan!

Eight-year-old Mariano and his family join us. It is Mariano and his little brother Robinson's first Yankees game. Very cool. I hope his namesake doesn't get traded or sign somewhere else. That could cause some family squabbles.

With the game moving closer and the ticket fiasco unfolding, friends from the past continue to arrive.

Through the crowd coming my way, I see a former classmate from Vero Beach High School class of 1988. Jimmy Assad and I were both into baseball and haven't seen each other since graduation. He saw on Facebook that I was going to be here. He offers his condolences on Jim and congrats on the *162* book. He doesn't really go by Jimmy anymore, but I continue to call him that since that is what I always called him as kids. His dad was the coach of the "major league" team in our area. Although both leagues were the same age, the major league team was a lot more competitive and traveled around to other cities.

One Florida afternoon, I was permitted a tryout that didn't go very well. In addition to not being able to hit the faster pitching, I also severely misjudged several fly balls. I wouldn't have made the Bad News Bears that day.

I remind Jimmy that at the end of practice his dad cut me and sent me back to the minor league team. I was devastated. I was 12 and remember crying uncontrollably when I got home. Jimmy listens and apologizes for me not making the team. The reality is that I wasn't as good as him and the rest of the team and we all have lessons to learn. I learned to deal with reality that day. Jimmy buys a *162* book and hands me a Yuengling. I'm sure he felt badly after I relay my life-direction changing story.

As game time nears, I call Mike over and tell him that despite the five bad tickets, we should be right at 42. At one point, I think Mike and I might have to scalp to get in. The Wanns show up and I have to tell them that I sold their tickets. I think they are relieved as they were just coming as a favor. They stay for the party.

We make our way in to the game. Today we are treated to David Price vs. CC Sabathia. Unfortunately the Rays are too much again and the Yanks lose again 4-2.

It is fun having everyone there, but exhausting. Three weeks after Jim's death and I am still experiencing a mix of shock, denial, and —sadly — acceptance.

I'm moving on but I don't want to.

Sunday, August 25

Its 9:45 a.m. already and I want to be set up with my book at Ferg's by 11 a.m.

The good news is that my hemorrhoids are vastly improving and have almost disappeared.

With no coffee in our systems, Mike and I begin our final quest to The Trop for the year. He is planning on dropping me off and heading on his four-hour drive home. I try to dissuade him as I do not have a ride to the airport or a place to stay.

Besides my morning flight to Toronto, I have nothing lined up for my trip to Canada — and I mean nothing. No tickets, lodging, or transportation.

No big deal.

I make a few calls to feel out the situation and look for a place to stay as Toronto is one of the most expensive road cities.

"Call Geri," Mike suggests.

"Is she still living in Toronto?"

He confirms that she is and within five minutes I have a downtown pad to crash in. The 162 guy is back in action. She tells me that for $3 I can take the Rocket bus, which connects to the subway, directly to her place. Two problems solved. No hotel and no rental car necessary. This will save me at least $700.

Problem solved for Toronto ... but what about tonight? It's a 30-minute/$70 cab ride to the airport, and I still have no place to stay. I decide to call my buddy Danny Vulin's cousin, Scott Oppel, who lives in the area. We ran into him at the game last night. I offer to buy his ticket to the game and his beers if he'll drive me after to an airport hotel.

"I'm golfing today, bro, but call me after the game if you haven't found a ride yet," he says.

Mike drops me off. I have all my luggage in Mike's car, and I do not travel lightly. I walk up to my usual spot in front of Ferg's and set up my books. Within a minute I am cornered by Jeff, yesterday's scalper.

"Well, that whole fiasco wound up costing me $100," he announces. "I had to reimburse $50 for the bad tickets, plus the sales I missed I could have made me another $50."

I hand him $75.

"Again, I really apologize," I offer. "How about we split the difference, and I agree to stay out of the ticket business down here in Florida?"

He laughs and seems content.

My focus now goes to buying a ticket for the Sunday matinee. I always say that it is all about supply and demand. There doesn't seem to be any tickets available and I don't want to have to go back to Jeff the scalper looking for a ticket. I sold 50 books yesterday, but today is much slower. I spot a woman haggling with Jeff as I move closer to eavesdrop.

"I'll give it to you for $50," she pleads.

"I don't buy singles," Jeff conveys with no interest.

"It includes all the pizza you can eat," she adds.

I wait until she walks away, as I don't want to poach on Jeff's territory.

"What do you got?"

She hands me a Papa John's bullpen ticket that includes food and non-alcoholic drinks.

"I paid $100, but I'll sell it for $50," she says.

I tell her that it doesn't matter what she paid, it is all about the current market.

After some hardcore negotiations we agree on $30 and an autographed *162* book.

I pack up a box of books and put my knapsack over my shoulder. I am in a hurry but soon realize that the game doesn't start at 1:00 p.m. but at 1:35. There is a huge sand castle inside the stadium to commemorate "The Sandman." I have been trying all weekend to see it.

I burrow my way up to the bar with all of my luggage and order a Yuengling. The couple next to me doesn't seem very happy that I am standing so close to them. This quickly gets compounded when my freshly poured Yuengling gets blindsided by my Yankee knapsack and violently tips the glass in their direction. They are immediately doused with beer. I offer napkins and an apology. When that fails, I pull out and autograph a *162* book and give them a copy. They still don't look happy, but at least I walk away feeling better.

The Rays are 74-53. The Yanks are 68-61. There are 33 to go, and today is a must-win. The sand sculpture is pretty amazing. Unfortunately, the likeness looks nothing like Mariano. Another city and another send-off for Number 42.

I walk down to my seat in the bullpen area and realize that it is general seating. I notice one seat that is available right in the front, and adjacent to the pitching mound off of right field. I settle in.

One of the only times I actually look better than "The Sandman."

"I must be in the front row," I say, mimicking Bob Uecker from the 1970's Miller Lite commercials, as I plop down next to a few Yankee fans. I am pleasantly surprised to see a full spread with salads and chicken in addition to the pizza.

The starting pitcher, Alex Cobb, is warming up. I am 10 feet from the 24-year-old who graduated from Vero Beach High, the same high school as Jim and I. The usher comes over and warns mostly the Yankee fans that any booing or other negative interaction is strictly prohibited.

"That's fine. You guys don't boo A-Rod and I won't

boo any of your players," I sternly retort.

I love going to baseball games. I immediately go from being exhausted and run down physically to being back on top of the world. The energy of the crowd feeds my feeble and hung-over body. That and a cold beer.

Today I am treated to another amazing baseball game. Alex Cobb has only given up more than three runs in two of his starts in 2013. Robinson Cano and Evan Longoria both tag solo shots today as the Rays go for the sweep. The Rays have won 16 of the last 21 against the Yanks at The Trop.

The score is knotted at 2-2. One of the things about baseball is that the games move slowly enough that you can "manage" along and second-guess certain decisions. In the top of the seventh, the Yankees have the bottom of the order coming up with Mark Reynolds (.213) and Chris Stewart (.226) before the pesky Brett Gardner.

Alex Rodriguez is not in the line up today and I yell out my frustration as Joe Girardi doesn't go to him to pinch hit against the lefty Jack McGee. I stand up and shout my advice. I often get frustrated with Girardi's moves ... or lack thereof.

"Come on, Joe! We are paying this guy $30 million. If you don't use him now, when are you going to use him? For Pete's sake, there is a lefty in there!"

McGee strikes out the side as one of the most feared hitters of the past two decades rests on the bench. Unbelievable.

The game heads into extra innings as David Robertson holds the Rays scoreless for two frames. In the 10th, Joe takes my advice and goes to A-Rod. Amazingly, I learn that he is 0 for 14 in his career coming off the pine. The boos get even louder as he connects for a hard single up the middle. The hit is wasted as a line drive doubles up Alex.

In the 11th, Soriano continues to make a difference as he scorches a double to left. Everyone in The Trop is surprised as the 38-year-old easily steals third. The Yanks grab the lead 3-2 as Curtis Granderson lifts a fly ball to center field.

Enter Sandman.

Mo trots out to the delight of the Florida crowd. He will face Zobrist, Longoria, and Joyce. I cheer with the rest of the crowd as we pay tribute to the legend. If you went to the bathroom you would have missed it. Six pitches (all strikes) is all it takes to record the final three outs and his 38th save.

Next stop, Toronto.

I have failed in my attempt to get a ride from strangers and call Scott back. He picks me up at Ferg's 45 minutes later and he drops me off at the Springhill Suites near the Tampa airport. He saved me at least $70, probably way more, as we sit on I-75 in Tampa traffic on a hot Sunday afternoon.

I fail in my attempt to avoid paying for a hotel, but work my magic and negotiate an $80 rate. I walk a few blocks to grab dinner and notice a gentlemen's club with a sign that reads, "Free drink with game tickets."

After my Sunday night conference calls, I fight off my boredom and morality issues and head out for some fun.

I decide to take them up on their offer and sit at the bar to collect my free drink. I save my game tickets from each game in case I ever have to prove that I was there to Guinness or whoever else wants to know.

The bartender delivers my Red Bull and vodka and snatches my Papa John's bullpen ticket. I try to argue that I need the ticket, but to no avail.

Every guy knows deep down that they will never get a stripper to leave with them. But we all try anyway. Tonight I am convinced that my "new friend" is the exception. With her Hungarian accent she tells me that she is so different from all the other girls and she does this because she loves to dance. Her real love is ballet. She says this as she twirls the hair on the back of my head with her fingers.

We trade interesting life stories and she seems to really be into me, while never looking at the time or trying to engage other customers.

After a solid hour of hanging out and getting to know each other, I have only bought her one drink. As her name is called for the main stage, she asks me if I would wait for her. I turn down several offers from the other girls even when the two-for-one lap dance special comes on.

I finally ask her for a dance and we make our way to the couches. As we wait for the next song, it is like the universe is messing with me. "Enter Sandman" begins to play.

> *Say your prayers little one*
> *Don't forget, my son*
> *To include everyone*
> *Tuck you in, warm within*
> *Keep you free from sin*
> *Till the Sandman he comes*
> *Sleep with one eye open*
> *Gripping your pillow tight*
> *Exit light*
> *Enter night*
> *Take my hand*
> *Off to Never Never Land*
> *Something's wrong, shut the light*
> *Heavy thoughts tonight*

And they aren't of snow white
Dreams of war, dreams of liars
Dreams of dragon's fire
And of things that will bite
Sleep with one eye open
Gripping your pillow tight
Exit light
Enter night
Take my hand
Off to Never Never Land
Now I lay me down to sleep
Pray the lord my soul to keep
If I die before I wake
Pray the lord my soul to take
Hush little baby, don't say a word
And never mind that noise you heard
It's just the beast under your bed,
In your closet, in your head
Exit light
Enter night
Grain of sand
Exit light
Enter night
Take my hand

We're off to Never Never Land

I smile to myself as I am the only one who gets the irony.

Three minutes later she whispers an invite to the VIP area where we can really have some fun.

"How much is that?" I ask cautiously.

"Only $300."

"Right. I'm going to have to pass."

She exits quickly.

And to think that I believed she liked me!

My little journey comes to an end as I walk out and make my way back to the hotel $35 lighter.

Off to Never Never Land.

Chapter Nine

MO SETS THE TONE

Monday, August 26

My flight for Toronto leaves at 8:30 a.m. and my wakeup call is for 6:00. This feels a lot like 2011 as I slumber into the bathroom. I am relieved that my hemorrhoids are improving daily.

My layover is in Detroit and I am talking Yankees baseball with the gentleman next to me at the bar who is from Connecticut. We weigh the Yankees chances this year and toast The Captain, Derek Jeter, who is making his return tonight.

I go to StubHub and chuckle as I see that I can get a ticket for $11. Upon checking out, I apply my StubHub $10 fancode coupon and my ticket tonight is a whopping $1.

I am seated at the corner of the bar during my two-hour layover, when the bartender informs me that the gentleman at the end of the bar is buying me a drink. I hold up my current beer that is almost empty and nod my appreciation.

"Who's on the back of your Yankees shirt?" he yells across a bar of travelers.

"162," I reply. "It's my own jersey."

He stands to show me that he is wearing 15 — the number of Thurman Munson, the great Yankees catcher from the 70s who died in a plane crash long ago. I gather my stuff and move to sit next to TJ from South Jersey and enjoy my free beer. I return the gesture with an autographed book. For the next hour, TJ and I talk about everything from the Yankees to, well, the Yankees! TJ thinks *The Last 42* tour is amazing and is happy to play a small part in it. The long, hard road continues to be made easier by fans that offer an encouraging word and validate my quest.

My flight arrives late in Toronto as I wait impatiently in the Customs line. At 4:45, I walk through the terminal exit and feel the warm Canada air. Geri has guided me through the public transportation system and I am looking for the Rocket bus. For $3 or (a looney and a tooney) I can make it all the way downtown. On my *162* tour, I took a taxi that ran me $60.

Geri's place is just a few minutes walk from the station. I roll my two large suitcases, one of which is packed with copies of 162, down several Toronto streets. I quickly change to my *162* jersey and we are off. We make it to the game by first pitch. My routine for the last 10 games is to carry a bag of books into the stadium.

Our first stop is to the nearest beer stand that sells decent beer. I step up to the front of the line and lay down two copies of *162* as I reach for my ID.

"What's the book about?"

"I'm the author. I attended all 162 Yankees games in 2011."

"My son would love this," she admits as she holds it up and checks it out. Her partner is pouring the beer.

"You are in luck," I tell her. "I do an employee discount for all stadium employees. They are $15 for everyone else. You can get one for $10."

"Will you autograph it?"

We finish the transaction and walk away. We have two fresh beers, her $10, and my $25 that I never handed over.

"That was easy," observes Geri.

"Yeah, and with all of the excitement of her getting the

book, they never charged us for the beer."

We look at each other.

"She'll have to pay for that at the end of the night," Geri offers with a hint of disappointment.

I'm not sure if Jim's watching my every move affected me or not, but I retreat back. I always like getting free stuff on my tour, but not at the expense of one of my customers. They are happy and surprised when I return a minute later with their $22 Canadian dollars.

The Captain returns tonight and is penciled in for just the sixth time in 2013.

Phil Hughes doesn't have his best stuff as NY goes down 5-2, dropping their third out of four, losing big to the last place Blue Jays.

At 10:45 a.m., my ride, Mark Trinidad, shows up. Mark is a comedy veteran and also works diligently building a LegalShield business. Mark has been doing stand up for 17 years and been with LegalShield for four. I have been doing stand up for four and LegalShield for 17. We both agree that it takes time to master something. In LegalShield, I'm the man — in comedy *he* is the man.

Over the last few years Mark has taken me under his wing. One of the things that I respect most about him is that he remembers where he comes from. He is humble and willing to help comics on their way up. While others might let their ego get in the way, he doesn't. He remembers where he came from.

I recently read in Mariano's book *The Closer* about one of Mo's minor league teammates, Tim Cooper. Tim and Mo would spend hours on long road trips teaching each other English and Spanish, respectively.

Every team needs a Tim Cooper. Here's an excerpt from *The Closer* featuring a conversation with Mariano Rivera early in his minor league career.

> *"Okay we're going to do a little role play right now,"* Coop says. *You just won Game 7 of the World Series, and Tim McCarver wants to talk to you. You can't call in a translator. That'll kill the moment. You have to be able to speak English, so you might as well start learning now. Ready?"*
>
> And Coop channels his best Tim McCarver.
>
> *"Mariano could you have imagined this when you were growing up in Panama — pitching in the World Series for the Yankees?"*
>
> *"Not really. It's amazing. Thanks to the Lord I was able to get those last outs."*
>
> *"You had to face three strong hitters at the end. What was your approach?"*
>
> *"I just want to make good pitches and get ahead."*
>
> *"You used to work on your father's boat, and now*

> you are a world champion. What have you learned along the way?"
>
> "I think if you have the help of the Lord, you can do anything. You can dream big things."

This was four years before Rivera would throw his first major league pitch and five years prior to him winning his first of five championships.

A year later, Coop and Mo are teamed up again single-A ball with the Greensboro Hornets in the South Atlantic league.

> The bigger challenge for me is off the field. I got off to a good start learning English, thanks to Coop, but unlike Tampa, Greensboro, NC is a place where almost nobody speaks my native language. It is a tremendously isolating. In restaurants and malls and convenience stores, my English shortcomings keep slamming into me.

One day in particular, Mo hits a breaking point as he leaves a store unable to communicate with the clerk.

> I don't know why it hits me in that moment, but it does. I feel like a sardine out of water, tangled in a net with no chance of escape. It feels really bad — completely overwhelming. I start to cry. I go to the bathroom and wash my face and look in the mirror. I turn out the light and go to bed. I am still crying.
>
> My linguistic pity party doesn't last long. I find Coop the next day.

> "I need to work on English, Coop. I am not doing good with it. I have to be able to talk when I win the World Series, right?"

Coop smiles.

> "We've got a lot of road trips left this year," he says. "You are going to be giving speeches by the time we're done."

> Tim Cooper is some teammate. He and I learn an awful lot on those long road trips, and not just the language.

Anyone and everyone who has crossed paths with Number 42 agrees that he is one of the nicest and most down-to-earth people. This is by design.

Mo recalls Tim saying:

> "If we ever make it to the top, let's make a deal that we are never going to big-league anybody," Coop says. "We're never going to act better than anybody or look down on anybody, because that is not what real big-leaguers do."

> "That's right," I say. "We don't big-league anybody. We stay humble. We remember where we came from."

> What's important is how you treat people. That's what really matters, right?" Coop says.

> Amen, Coop.

> *This simple truth becomes a beacon for how to live life for me, in baseball and out of baseball. The Lord doesn't care about wealth or fame or the number of saves somebody has. We are all children of God, and the Lord cares about the goodness and love in our hearts. That's all.*

None of this surprises me about Mo. This is part of the fabric of what makes him a great man. I recall a *Sports Illustrated* article that demonstrated this idea perfectly.

Mo decided that he wanted his legacy to be about more than baseball. So he decided that in each city he traveled to in his last season, he wanted to meet people who had dedicated their lives to baseball or had come across some great illness or tragedy. Mo met with one family that had a flight-display board weighing more than 300 lbs. fall on them at the airport. Their 10-year-old son, Luke, was killed. The mom had suffered two broken legs and the dad suffered a broken leg and head injuries.

When Mo walked into the room, the family's demeanor changed. He huddled with the hurting family and offered his love and support. Luke was an avid baseball fan ... but he hated the Yankees! When Mo learned this, he laughed along with the family and offered these words:

> *"Luke will always be with you. There is a plan for everything. We don't always know what it is, but we have to keep putting one step forward at a time.*

> My situation is nowhere near what you are going through. I had an injury right here in Kansas City and overcame it to play again. My only message is you have to keep on trying and keep on giving effort."

Luke's little brother had a further request of Mo. He asked if he could have the ball from the last out of the game that evening. When the game was finally over, the family waited around for a while, but having to navigate wheelchairs back toward the Yankees dugout seemed to daunting, so they decided to pack it up and leave. When they got to their parking spot, a representative from the Kansas City Royals called them and asked them to come back into the stadium ... because Mo was frantically looking for them to give them the promised baseball.

Six weeks later, it dawns on Mo that he never autographed that ball, so he got in touch with the family, had them send him the ball for him to sign, and then he sent it back. That's class. That's Mo. One of a kind.

We arrive at a networking lunch. The 25 in attendance all get a chance to stand up and promote themselves and their businesses. I do a LegalShield overview, while promoting my *162* book and *The Last 42* tour. I give away one copy as a door prize and sell 10 more after lunch. I'm getting closer to a million as I sell my 2,000th book by lunchtime.

I post on Facebook that I am looking for a ticket tonight. I get several offers for people to buy me a ticket online including my friend Scott Osbourne from Scotland. My *162* readers may recall that he was one of the funnier characters that I ran into in Detroit in what I refer to as the "trunk incident." Not only did he buy me a playoff ticket when I needed one, he also recently donated $500 to our foundation, Work, Play, Love.

I get a text from Jim's friend, Georgia. "You have a ticket in a skybox tonight at the Rogers Centre!" Nice! I also receive offers for tomorrow from another friend, Lindsey Myers. "How about Wednesday? I got you a ticket." So I get into all three games for $1. I could do this for a living. Oh, Canada!

Game 12 is in the books, as the Yanks win 10-3. A-Rod hits his second homerun in as many days. Eleven down and 31 to go.

Chapter Ten

CREATURE FEATURES

Thursday, August 28

Today I add doing laundry to my list. I put in a load as I wait next door and enjoy a cold beer and make some phone calls. When I did *162*, I barely worked my LegalShield business. I promised my partners that I would be way more connected this time around.

In addition to the ticket from my friend Lindsey, I get a call from Jeff Sammut from 590 The Fan's Sportsnet. I have been on his radio show twice and we have stayed in touch. He says that if I can meet him immediately he has two tickets for me. Coincidently enough, his office is two blocks from where I am. I quickly fold my laundry, neatly repack my suitcase, and wheel down to the street in downtown Toronto. Three free tickets tonight!

Geri and a newer associate, Anita Sardo, are the recipients of my good fortune. Unfortunately, none of it has rubbed off on Yankees starter Hiroki Kuroda. Kuroda had been dominant in July (3-0, 0.55 ERA), but that's not the case anymore. The 38-year-old permitted nine hits on Wednesday and has allowed 15 earned runs in his last 16 2/3 innings (8.10 ERA), falling to 1-4 this month.

He gets lit up like a Christmas tree in Rockefeller Center and takes his third beating in a row. He was — *was* being the key word — the hottest pitcher in the American League. The Yanks drop four of six. During the 2011 season, I could always say, "No big deal, it's a long season." But I don't have that luxury now.

With his club in jeopardy of not making the playoffs for just the second time in 19 seasons, Manager Joe Girardi knows the results of the road trip are not making the task any simpler. The loss drops New York 5 ½ games behind the Athletics for the second American League Wild Card spot.

I am glad to be back at the stadium with a 10-game home stand in front of us. I take advantage of the travel day and get caught up on errands, promotion, and logistics for the rest of the tour. Welcome back to the grind. We will play every day over the next 17. No days off. A 10-game home stand followed by trips to Baltimore and Boston, which I will drive to.

The Orioles are in town this weekend and there is a playoff feel in Da Bronx. The O's, with a 71-61 record, hold a 1½-game lead over the Yankees who are 70-63.

The Bombers take the first two games of the Labor Day series to inch in front of Baltimore and move into third place for the remaining Wild Card spot. Mariano picks up his 39th save on Friday night while Nova goes the distance Saturday in a three-hit complete game shutout.

Sunday, September 1

My nephew Shane pulls up to the house right on time. He has recently returned from a year-long trip to China. Shane and I are a lot alike and I always enjoy his company. He fills me in on some of his Asian adventures as we are off to Manhattan to pick up an old friend from New Jersey, Katarina. The Greek actress and I used to "hang out" when I was in my early 20s. I haven't seen her in years, but thanks to Facebook we have reconnected. Katarina is terrified of taking the subway, so we have to stop in NYC at Port Authority. This is a major inconvenience, but that's what friends are for.

Yankee fans are treated to vintage Andy Pettitte in Da Bronx on this gorgeous Sunday. The Yanks are cruising towards a sweep as Pettitte has a 3-0 lead in the seventh. Joe Girardi gives him the hook after two lead-off singles and just 93 pitches. Interesting move. I am seated with The Creatures today, and the natives are getting restless.

Shawn Kelley comes in and it doesn't take long to undo Andy's masterpiece. Four pitches to be exact. Matt Wieters singles, followed by a first-pitch J.J. Hardy homerun, and the Orioles take a 4-3 lead. It gets worse. Boone Logan replaces Kelley and gives up a walk and a single. Girardi walks to the mound and signals for Joba Chamberlain. You have got to be kidding me.

The boos follow from the Yankee Stadium crowd. I'm not sure if we are booing Kelley, Joba, Logan, Girardi, or just the 2013 season in general. Either way, I show my disgust and join the other fans as Chamberlain puts the game out of reach as he offers up an 83 mph slider that Adam Jones launches straight away into Monument Park.

After the Yankee bullpen blows the lead, we make our way up to the bar. Shane can handle his beer pretty well. I can't say as much for Katarina. She is having a blast and doesn't want it to end. It's the holiday weekend and she wants the party to go late into the night. Tomorrow is Labor Day and our third straight day game. *The Last 42* guy needs to pace himself.

The head bartender at the dugout is Becca. She is quick to recognize me and greets me with a hug. I autograph a book for her and one for the general manager, Louis.

These two were constants in my life in 2011 and it is amazing to see them. Louis won't accept my gift and insists that I take $20. Becca tells me to come back tomorrow and she will help me sell some books to the regulars.

Later that night, I post on Facebook: *Looking for tickets to ANY of the remaining Yankees games. Go to the game with me and you are in the next book,* The Last 42. *Any takers?*

Monday, September 2 - Labor Day

We are 3½ out of the second Wild Card spot with 26 games to go. I am 10-6 on my trip. I am being accepted as a Creature. My daily routine for home games is definitely different than my 162 tour. It includes meeting a lot more people and drinking a lot less beer.

If you have been to Yankee Stadium over the last decade you may have noticed a young man named Freddy in his motorized wheelchair. He has a severe case of muscular dystrophy and zips up and down River Ave. selling candy. What people probably don't see are his daily stops in front of Bald Vinny's House of Tees. He uses his one functioning hand to operate the wheelchair. He rolls up every home game to Vinny and George. They have a daily chat about life and their favorite team.

The Last 42

Vinny, *no matter what he is doing,* stops, pulls away, and makes time for Freddy.

Milano then pulls out his candy from a secret compartment and helps the salesman get ready for business. He takes his Yankees hat out of Freddy's bag and secures it on his head and sends him off with smile and a kind word. I glance over to see George leaning over for his daily pep talks with Freddy.

Of all the things I witness in this crazy world every day, watching these tough New Yorkers and Bleacher Creatures seems to make everything OK. It's hard not to have tears in my eyes as I reflect on how important it is to help and be nice to others. Especially those who might appear to be less fortunate.

Just as he does with everyone, Vinny makes Freddy feel included and important.

Just before game time, Freddy changes from selling candy to looking for a single ticket. Not unlike me. He gets a ticket every night, most of the time for free.

For years I have seen him and avoided him in his severely handicapped state. Not anymore. Now I make a point to say hi and do whatever I can to brighten his day.

Today, he has his mom with him. I call her over and hand her a *162* book. Watching Freddy every day not even blink at his own challenges should serve as a life lesson for anyone lucky enough to cross his path.

"How long has Freddy been selling candy out here?" I ask Bald Vinny today.

"Whew ... longer than I've been selling t-shirts. For years."

Another fixture on River Ave., is NYPD's Wayne Townsend. He is way more friendly than he is intimidating. Over the last few weeks he has come to recognize me as he makes his stroll down River Ave. He always has time for everyone and his smiles are as genuine as his handshakes are firm.

"So tell me about your book," he implores.

As I begin to share my journey, he starts shaking his head.

"Are you serious? All 162? That must have been amazing!"

His eyes never leave me as I hold up my book and my face lights up as I always do when talking of the record-breaking streak.

He pulls out his wallet. "I'm not a Yankees fan at all. I'm Mets all the way, but I gotta read this."

"Your money is no good here, Wayne," I say with a grin as I give one of NY's finest a fresh copy.

He accepts graciously and keeps moving along River Ave., making his habitual greetings down the line.

Today I leave at 9:30 a.m. for a 1 p.m. game. It takes me 45 minutes to get to the stadium. I drop my stuff off in front of Billy's Sports Bar. I have learned first-hand this weekend that the game's outcome controls the sales climate. We win, people buy. We lose, people rush home.

I enter The Dugout as I did almost daily in 2011. Becca points and yells across the bar, "There he is!" She yells to three fans in the corner of the bar as I put down my 20-lb. bag on the bar.

"Do you guys remember two years ago a couple of guys who went to every game ..."

A taller guy with a bandana interrupts her.

"Wait, I know this story." He turns to me empathetically, "Did you have a brother who passed away recently?"

I begin to nod.

"I read your story in

At The Dugout with Becca

The Post a few weeks ago. I'm Motorcycle Pete." (*Bald Vinny, 162 Guy, Motorcycle Pete* ... In case you hadn't noticed, monikers are big in the Bronx.)

We shake hands. Pete and I bond quickly. He is a huge Yankees fan and The Dugout is his second home. I also quickly recognize another guy from two years ago that Steve Marcinowski (Marz) and I actually interviewed while we were still making a movie. Marz started the 162 journey with me in 2011 and attended 57 games with me.

"I'm Ray. This is my wife Terry," he reminds me.

"I remember you," I reply.

"What happened to your buddy?"

"It's a long story."

"And a *good* story," Becca chimes in. "I started reading it last night. Thanks for the shout-outs." She plops down a tall boy PBR in front of me.

"Put that on my tab," insists Motorcycle Pete.

I can't make change and sign books fast enough. Pete and Ray and a few other customers get caught up in the action. I sell more books at The Dugout today than I did at my table. Maybe I should rethink my strategy.

Pete shows some pictures of his bike that is decked out with Yankee memories from the past.

"What are you doing for tickets? We always have extras," Pete announces to the delight of my tickling ears. He and I exchange numbers and agree to stay in touch.

I have been starting all of the games in section 203 with The Creatures. Roll Call continues to be one of my favorite parts of the day. This is a tradition that only the NY Yankees embrace.

To begin each game, Bald Vinny starts with a loud yelping of sorts. He starts in center field with the entire Section 203 standing quietly and waiting.

"Currrrrrrrrtissss!" he screams from the depth of his soul.

Then The Creatures follow his cue, "Cur-tis, (clap,clap,) Cur-tis," until the player acknowledges them. They then move to left to Brett Gardner. "I-chi-ro, I-chi-ro," is chanted next to the right fielder. Then it's the infield from first to third.

For Yankees fans, this is a must. Make your way to 203 and sit as close to Bald Vinny as possible. He's easy to spot. He's bald, wearing a Creatures shirt, smiling, and wearing dark wraparound shades. I don't usually have seats in 203, but today I have scalped one from Joel, another Creature faithful. The bleacher seats are $20 for the season ticket holders.

Udi is probably my favorite of all The Creatures. Probably because he has always been the nicest to me. He is a fixture in 203 and is never far from Bald Vinny.

He can always tell when I am out of the loop as to Creature traditions and does his best to make me feel included.

For instance, when something really good happens, The Creatures do three consecutive fist pumps. No high fives. Fist pumps, three of them. I do it, but quite frankly, it is a little awkward.

Joel brought his own bagged lunch today and offers me half of his sandwich. I decline, but am touched nonetheless. Who does that? He asks what they are doing on the upcoming day off. There is a Staten Island game, which is the Yankees minor league team and invites everyone to go. That is hardcore. Apparently, 81 home games isn't enough. It is the closest thing that I can remember to being part of a fraternity. A group of people who come together for a reason or a cause, when they seemingly have nothing else in common.

Another game within the game is to guess who will hit the first Yankees homerun.

There are four or five Creatures who usually play. The oldest Creature gets to choose first. Today Joel chooses Granderson. Udi goes with Soriano. Vinny always picks Cano. Another creature picks A-Rod. I cough up my $5 to play and choose Mark Reynolds. Some raise their eyebrows, while Udi declares, "There is a first. I don't think anyone has ever picked Reynolds."

Anyone who has ever spent more than a minute in the bleachers knows The Queen, Tina. I don't think she knew me two years ago, but is really nice to me now. She stops by my table every day and says hello. I think The Queen may be a sarcastic nickname, because she is tough. Bronx tough. She probably knows more about the history of the Bleacher Creatures than anyone. She isn't afraid to tell you about it, either. She is stocky with curly blond hair and tough as nails. I'm glad I'm on her good side.

The Yanks cruise today 9-1 as the game is interrupted by a two-hour rain delay. Jeter heats up, going 2-4 with two batted in. There are no homeruns in this one though, as I break even in my first Creature wager.

Chapter Eleven

RANDOM AXE OF KINDNESS

Tuesday, September 3

I pull up to the FDNY academy in Fort Totten to carpool with my brother, the chief. Fort Totten is a huge facility spread over 55 acres and 50 buildings. I enjoy hanging with the FDNY brass, but even more so spending time with my big brother.

Danny and I are seated in the first row of 326. Danny sees a guy keeping score and engages him in conversation.

"This is my baby brother, he went to every game in 2011, all 162."

Within three minutes I have sold another book. The lady next to me overhears and she forks over $15 as well and buys her 34-year-old son a birthday present.

If I had Dan with me at every game, I'd be rich.

The game has been going along with a 1-1 tie until Chicago explodes with three runs in the 5th.

I get a Facebook message from Becki Schick. You may recall I met Becki, a very attractive young lady, a couple of weeks ago when she approached me and offered her condolences for Jim. She had read about me in the *NY Post* article. We became Facebook friends, and I was happy to hear from her.

Hey there- I saw your post about tickets. I don't need any credit (I'm pretty low key) but for the rest of this week I have

With my brother, Batallion Chief Dan Melia

an extra ticket for tomorrow and Sunday. Let me know if you want it for either game (but again- low key)

I message her back right away.

You rock! I am set for tomorrow - but I'd love Sunday - I really appreciate it :)

She replies.

You got it! I'll just see you on the Ave and give it to you then! Glad to help- and besides- I almost always have an extra ticket (I can't give them away!!) BTW -you are going to love these seats They are in 103."

I quickly show my phone to Dan. "How about this?" I show him a picture of my new friend as well.

"Wow, she's cute. You have some scam going," he laughs.

The two tickets that I do have for tomorrow were comps from the rainout. I immediately regret my decision to only take Sunday. Within eight minutes of my original acceptance, I get back on Facebook and I say that I have changed my mind and would love Wednesday as well. What was I thinking? Since it was only eight minutes, amazingly they are still open. Very Cool! I am just as stoked to sit with her. Besides me, she is probably the most normal Yankees fanatic I have met.

With the score 4-1, Chris Sales is on the mound for the

White Sox and continues to baffle the batters. Dan and I keep an eye on his pitch count. The only way to beat Sales is to outlast him. My brother is a great guy to watch sports with as he is into every pitch as much as I am. Sales has his A-game today. Our only chance is getting into that bullpen. We enter the bottom of the 8th with only three hits and Sales' pitch count is 102.

After a one out Jeter single, Cano rips a double to the wall. The Stadium is rocking. It is good to see fight in the Yankees. Sales is removed and the fun continues. Soriano drives in both runners with a single up the middle as the Yanks close the gap to 4-3. A-Rod moves him over with another single. Curtis Granderson delivers a pinch hit double scoring A-Rod and tying the game. An out later, Nunez delivers the go-ahead RBIs, sending the Yanks on top for the first time tonight, 6-4.

Enter Sandman. Mariano comes in and makes quick work of Chicago and earns his 40th save of his last season. Forty and we still have almost a month to go. I believe he can reach 50. He could also probably go another five years.

Wednesday, September 4

Tonight is the final game of the White Sox series. I am really looking forward to sitting with Becki and sort of nervous. Like schoolgirl nervous. Butterflies. I'm sure that she is just being nice, but I can't help getting nervous around someone as beautiful as Becki.

I am not exactly sure what she meant by "low key," but I'm guessing that she doesn't want me thanking her all over Facebook. So I don't. I also am careful not to mention it to any Creatures. I don't need my new circle of friends teasing us in any way. Through casual Facebook browsing (not stalking), I learn that Becki seems pretty normal. In one post she refers to Yankee Stadium as her "Happy Place." I like that.

She arrives on the Ave. with hugs for all of the regulars. She is the kind of person who brightens the area. She walks up and rips apart two tickets, handing me one. For someone who interacts with people every day, I am very jittery.

George raises his eyebrows and smiles my way. Becki and I agree to meet inside. George moves closer to my table. "You have some operation going," he whispers.

"Yeah I actually already had tickets today, but I couldn't pass up 103," I reply.

"Right. Or sitting with Becki," he correctly assesses.

"Yeah, let's not make a big deal out of that. I don't want you guys teasing her ... and blowing it for me."

Becki's section are field-level seats located directly behind the right fielder and in front of the Bleacher Creatures. She has a 40-game package, which is a quarter of the season, or half of the home games. We are alike in many ways and very different as well. I think she may be the kindest person I have ever met. She pulls out a ball when we first sit and tells me of her strategy to give it to a deserving kid.

She makes a comment about how amazing it is that people go so crazy for a ball and how you can use it to put a smile on a kid's face. I review my own behavior and laugh to myself at my own wacky aspirations to get a ball. While I would do almost anything to *get* a ball — for the memory and for the story — Becki will do anything to *give one away* ... for the same reasons.

As I sit next to this high-spirited, professional woman with the same fanatical tastes as mine, I think about Jim and how I should be learning more about giving from this young lady. Although I do many philanthropic events to support our foundation, this is different. Simple random acts of kindness with no other motives.

I pull out a bottle of water and hand it to her. "You have to stay hydrated."

"Good choice in water," she replies. I later learn that she works for Nestle.

She proceeds to give me some background on our section. The beer vendor, "Brewski," comes down the aisle and makes sure that he gives Becki a big hello.

She buys the first round and doesn't even touch her Bud Light. She tells me that she just likes to support him. According to Becki, Brewski has worked here more than 40 years and is the 17th employee with tenure. She is like a walking Yankees encyclopedia.

In the bottom of the first, a Robinson Cano homerun goes directly over our heads into 203. I'm guessing Bald Vinny just won a few bucks.

Halfway through the game and following the pre-inning warm ups, center fielder Brett Gardner identifies a young boy in the first row and throws the ball right to him. Unfortunately, it floats over his head to a guy a few rows back. It happens a good 30 feet away to our right, but Becki is quick to her feet. She starts yelling as if the ump blew a call in game seven of the World Series.

"That ball was meant for the kid. Give it to him!" she demands. She shakes her head in disbelief as she remains standing with her hands on her hips. "Can you believe that? That guy knew that Gardner was throwing it to the kid!" For the next inning she keeps looking over in their direction, shooting daggers at them through her steely gaze. She then disappears for a while and I see her pop up in the front row and present the young Yankees fan with a ball.

Becki is "low key" and she'll probably punch me for telling this story, but I'll take my chances. Turns out she went to the gift shop and purchased an official MLB ball for $32. Here's the kicker. She then scuffs the ball up with dirt and who knows what else so the kid won't think that she bought it. She didn't tell me, but I'm sure that she snuck a dirty look to the fan with the Gardner ball when she walked by.

Having a ball with Becki

I also learn that one of her pet peeves is people sitting where they do not belong. So I stay quiet regarding some of my tricks about seat jumping. She has a 40-game package with $80 tickets. That breaks down to $6,400 for the season. Yikes. She's probably not that interested in how I get in for $20 or less almost every night and sneak around to the better seats.

Becki displays another example of chivalry with two fans to our left. There is a cameraman in our section and Becki realizes that the two fans are about to be on the Jumbotron. She scrambles for her phone and snaps a picture of them on the big screen.

"People never get a picture of themselves up there, because it happens so fast," she explains. She then takes off and plops down by these two complete strangers. She gets their phone number and texts them the picture. How cool is that? Imagine if everyone was a little more like Becki. I am inspired and honestly never met anyone as kind as her.

I want to be clear that she seems to be like this *all of the time*. She is in no way trying to get in the next book or show off her giving spirit. At one point, she takes off and comes back with a huge plate of steak and two forks, "Hope you are hungry. I can't eat all of this." I'm not sure if she thinks I'm broke and homeless or if she is just this generous.

CC Sabathia and the Yanks go into the 8th up 6-1 and it looks like the Mariano will get a much-needed night off, with Boston coming in for four.

Not so fast. After 111 pitches and runners on first and second with one out, Girardi goes to Robertson. Three hits and a walk later and the Yankees are barely clinging onto a 6-5 lead.

Every game is like the playoffs now. Becki's seats are adjacent to the Yankees bullpen. We watch Mariano Rivera warm up and trot out to the mound. The Panamanian gets the final four outs and his 41st save as the Yanks complete a three-game sweep of the White Sox.

Tonight I made a new friend and learned firsthand about the power of random acts of kindness.

Thursday, September 5

The Bombers are 5-1 on the home stand and Yankees fans are buying books. It's a good thing I listened to Bald Vinny and didn't quit.

Like most Yankees fans, my heart beats a lot faster when the Red Sox come to town. The Thursday night crowd is pumped for September baseball and hosting Boston for four important games.

I get a text from Motorcycle Pete.

Stop in the dugout and I'll buy you a beer. BTW- Read most of your book during the commercials the last two nights. Love it!

I'm glad to oblige and go and hang out with Motorcycle Pete.

Yankees and Red Sox fans have not been cheated out of exciting games through the years. Tonight is no exception. The seventh inning stretch and "Take Me Out to the Ballgame" are only dampened by the fact that the Yankees are down 7-2. Yankees fans are hoping that their bats have a rally in them. Ichiro walks. Pinch hitter Vernon Wells singles. Brett Gardner singles. The Yankees fans know that anything is possible when Boston comes to town.

Now down 7-3, Jeter earns a walk and brings the tying run to the plate in Robinson Cano. A force-out scores a run and leaves the Bombers with first and third and one out. 7-4 Boston. Soriano keeps the party going as the stadium erupts on a single to left bringing Gardner home. 7-5. The Grandy Man is next. He rockets a fastball in the right field corner. 7-6.

A "Let's go Yan-kees," chant fills the new stadium. Games like this are like a drug. I can't get enough.

A-Rod strikes out swinging for the second out. Lyle Overbay steps up to do some damage against his former team. He does just that. The rally continues with a single to left scoring Soriano and Granderson. 8-7 Yankees. Wow. That was amazing! David Robertson trots in and takes the mound to pitch the eighth. The Yankees future closer makes quick work of Boston. He strikes out Ellsbury and Victorino. Dustin Pedroia grounds out to The Captain at short and we move to the ninth as Robertson lowers his ERA to 1.85.

Usually that would be the end of the story. Mariano Rivera comes in for save number 42. The greatest closer of all time quickly records the first two outs on just eight pitches.

I collect my book of bags and head for the exit. I have been getting better at timing my departure without missing anything important. I make it up to the turnstile as Mike Napoli slaps a single off the edge of his bat.

Uh oh.

The Red Sox tie the game, sending Mariano to the showers as they win it the 10th while handing Joba Chamberlain the loss.

Saturday, September 7

Part of my daily routine now is to pack up a little early and head over to The Dugout. Becca has been one of my best 162 promoters. I walk into The Dugout 20 minutes before the first inning and she gives her normal big hello with a smile. It doesn't take her long to help me sell a few books.

I'm having a friendly conversation with my new customers, two ladies from upstate. With the rivalry due to start any minute, I am finishing up my $3 PBR and preparing to head in. For some reason, I feel compelled to ask her what she does for a living. "We are teachers," she says joyfully.

Although I am in a hurry to make my way into Yankee Stadium, I pause, reflect on what Jim would do, and decide to stay and engage.

"What do you teach?"

"Special Ed."

"So, I'm working on a new book project. My inspiration this time was my brother Jim. He was an educator down in Florida and we lost him about a month ago suddenly to a heart attack."

"I'm so sorry."

"Thanks. Actually the last month has been an incredible experience. I just wanted you to know that whether you know it or not — you are making a big difference in these kids' lives. Teachers are special people. You are appreciated and respected."

I order another PBR and a round of vodka cranberries for my new friends. We raise our drinks and do a toast to teachers — the real heroes. I proceed to tell her about Jim, the memorial, the funeral, and all of the people who came up to me and shared.

We chat for a few more minutes and I am on my way. As I cross River Ave. and make my way to the bleacher entrance, I wipe away a tear and look up to the sky as I have done many times in the last few weeks. Still hard to believe.

I make my way to Section 124 and use a ticket from

earlier in the week to get in. The usher knows me by now and doesn't even look at my ticket.

With the Bombers getting bombed 12-3 and the hot sun beaming down, I throw in the towel and head for the Jack Daniels bar in the air conditioning. I place two *162* books on the bar and —wallah! — I get drinks bought for me a few minutes later. The bartender buys a book and I trade her another one for a $15 sangria.

Pinstripe Maniac Manny Man stops by and we watch an inning together on the big screen. We met on the Maniac site and we have become friends as he stops by my table before most home games to say hello. The cool thing about this year is that I'm starting to meet a lot of new friends. It's nice to have someone to commiserate with during these blowouts.

The Yankees threaten to come back, but fall short as the Boston slaughter continues and we take yet another beating, 13-9. In the first three losses, Boston pounds out 50 hits and scores 34 runs.

Sunday, September 8

"My boss thinks I am way too nice. In fact, he thinks that I am crazy." This is game two with Becki, and I am moving my head back and forth watching the game and listening intently.

"On Friday, I was running a little late as I'm driving into the office and it was drizzling. With hot rollers in my hair, I see the bus, and out of the corner of my eye I see a lady dressed in a skirt suit with sneakers running to catch the bus. I keep thinking, 'She's never going to make it.' Without hesitation, I roll the window down, and ask her, 'Do you want a ride?' To my surprise, she says, 'Yes!' and starts to get in! The bus was still up ahead. I tried to catch the bus at the next stop, but didn't make it. So now I have a complete stranger in my car. I just simply ask her where she needed to go because I'm fully committed at this point. Lucky for me, she was going to the Tarrytown train station, so it was only about 15-20 minutes out of my way."

I laugh as Becki animatedly recalls the adventure while we take in another ballgame on a beautiful September afternoon.

"I told this to my boss, and he was like, 'You are nuts. You are going to meet a psycho that way ... or an axe murderer!'

"Who is the crazy one?" she asks. "Not me. It's obvious that the woman was late for work or a meeting. She was dressed in a suit. I think that *she* is the crazy one for getting in the car of a complete stranger!"

With that, Becki sees Brewski. She pays for our beers, hands Brewski a big tip, and launches back in. I am trying to look attentive ... but not too attentive like I am remembering this for a book or anything.

"Was your boss mad that you were late?"

"No." She stops and looks at me. "You are missing the point. The point is that he thinks I was being way too nice."

I tell her that I think it is refreshing when people are kind. I truly feel like Becki is here to teach me some lessons. My mom used to say it best: "It's nice to be nice."

There are certain people who make the extra effort to make the path for others more enjoyable. Becki's kindness is no accident. Born into a half-Italian family, her earliest recollections are of her aunt and her parents continually giving to others. In her 20s, Becki made a New Year's resolution to pay a compliment to at least one person every single day. Becki lives by the rule that you never know when someone is having a bad day or going through a hard time ... so why not just be nice? The people you're nice to today will hopefully pay it forward, and before you know it, you've cultivated a culture of kindness.

In the meantime, we are hoping that the gods of kindness will smile on the Yankees on this day, as they are trying to avoid an embarrassing sweep. Becki and I debate whether Mariano will come in and pitch two innings again. With the season on the line, the gate opens and Mariano makes another early entrance. The Yanks take the Sunday game to avoid the sweep.

Kindness, indeed.

Chapter Twelve

BOSTON STRONG

Monday, September 9

Once a year, around the anniversary of 9/11, FDNY hosts a NY sports celebrity breakfast. It was one of the highlights of my 2011 odyssey. Danny brings me as his date once again.

Much like two years ago, I awake at 5:30 a.m. I follow my brother, Hyper Dan, through traffic all the way to Brooklyn. We arrive at the FDNY headquarters and drop off my car.

"Let's go in have a cup of coffee," he says. "A few of the officers want to meet the *162* guy."

They treat me like a hero, which seems backwards. I suppose it's a good thing, though. Everyone has a dream. Many books and speakers will teach people how to go after your dreams. I was simply an example. If my story can inspire one person then it was all worth it. Who am I kidding? It was worth every minute!

For my entire life the FDNY has been an important part of my story. My dad was a deputy chief when I was born and retired as a battalion chief. I was honored to sit with a few of New York City's bravest. Danny has done a great job of spreading the word about 162 and these guys are enthralled. They offer their sympathy for Jim as pictures of him are plastered around the chief's desk.

We drive his Department-issued car through Manhattan and are allowed to park wherever we want. We arrive at the historic NYC Athletic Club and I've got my usual knapsack full of books. The first person we meet is a sharply dressed guy on the elevator.

"You going up to the breakfast?" asks Danny with his hearty smile and firm handshake.

"Yes, Marty Appel," the guy introduces himself.

"Chief Melia. This is my baby brother. He wrote a book on going to every Yankee game in 2011."

The gentlemen coyly smiles, "I have a special interest in the Yankees as well."

He stops there as the Commissioner, the Department Chief, and a few others in uniform squeeze in. The elevator gets to our floor and the conversation ends there.

"That names sounds familiar," Dan whispers to me. "Find out who he is."

We later learn that Marty was the PR person for the Yankees in the '70s and has written several books on the storied franchise.

I get reacquainted with the Department Chief, Ed Kilduff, and the Commissioner, Sal Cassano. Danny reminds them of my 162 journey and brings them up to date on my book and *The Last 42* tour. Kilduff is a class act who is easy to talk to.

"What is your favorite stadium?" he asks.

"I love going to Fenway," I tell him. "It is so intense there."

He proceeds to tell me a story about his wife and his last trip to Fenway Park. I pull out a fresh 162 book and address it to Chief Kilduff.

Each table has a sports celebrity and ours has former Giants punter Sean Landeta sitting two seats on my left. He takes his two Super Bowl rings out of a special case and passes them counter-clockwise around the table. I am soaking this up and enjoying it as much as anyone. What could be better than hanging out with the FDNY brass and NY sports celebrities? A fanatic's dream. I snap a few pictures and make my way around as much as I can.

Commissioner Sal Cassano opens up and gives us a "state of the union" address of the FDNY. He introduces Mike Francesa, the afternoon voice of WFAN. Francesa is behind the podium and, after some brief statements, opens up for sports-related questions. I quickly raise my hand a few times and finally get the floor.

"What do you think about Mariano coming in during the 8th inning again yesterday? And — part two — do the Yankee have a chance at the playoffs?"

"Who else you gonna put in?" he asks rhetorically. He goes through the woes of the Yankees bullpen and then says it will take an absolute miracle for the Yankees to make the playoffs.

Afterwards we get to meet again as brother Dan reintroduces us and I give him an autographed copy of *162*. Just like two years ago, my older brother whisks me around to all the celebrities.

Next up is Mets catcher Anthony Recker. My brother is speaking with him as I walk up. He points to me.

"This is my baby brother that I was telling you about. He's going to all of the Mets games next."

"Really?" Recker asks incredulously.

"No," I laugh, "But everything's negotiable."

He is very cool and says that he is looking forward to reading the book. I also get to meet two new basketball players in New York, Mason Plumlee of the Nets and Knicks center John Wallace.

The FDNY put their lives on the line every day and it is nice to watch them kick back and enjoy themselves. I grab a few FDNY hats on the way out. After losing Jim, I'm enjoying hanging out with Dan as much as any of the stars that we just met. Life is short. We all need to spend time with our loved ones.

I'm exhausted as I get in my car and head down I-95 to Baltimore for a four-game must-win series. My brother Mike is on his way from Florida to take in some of the series. Sixteen games to go, and only one game out of the Wild Card.

After a couple of quick games in Baltimore, Rivera earns saves number 42 and 43, and picked up his sixth win to boot. He also breaks his own record as he notches number 650 for his storied career. **Both the Rays and the Rangers have lost, so our hopes are still alive as we move back into within two games of the last Wild Card spot.**

I get a chance to go to a game with my cousin, John Ziemblicki, and his wife Cheryl. John and Jim were best friends growing up. They played basketball together and John's dad, who was a NYPD cop, was their coach. He may have been the coolest uncle ever. He took Jim and I and his kids to see "Ghostbusters." I remember him saying to me, "I love laughing at the movies. Life can be so depressing. Why would I want to pay for that, when I get it everyday?"

Every game I go to with someone who knew Jim, the conversation leads to how and why Jim made an impact or what they remember. It makes me feel closer to him.

Friday, September 13

Much like two years ago, I am driving through the night to Boston. In 2011, thanks to Hurricane Irene, there were no hotel rooms anywhere and I slept in my car. *162* readers may recall that I was nearly arrested by Connecticut state police for "allegedly" breaking into cars in the hotel parking lot. This time I drive just two hours and grab a cheap room. I sleep exactly four hours and head to Logan International to pick up Ashley. She's in town for the Friday and Saturday games and then Mike is meeting me for Mo's final game at Fenway Sunday night.

Thinking Mariano's final games at Fenway would be a tough ticket, I lined them up in advance for the Saturday game ($269 for two) and Sunday ($479 for four.)

Supply and demand. I log into StubHub from my hotel room and buy two tickets for tonight for $24.

Ashley is fun and is always an adventure. I warn her that Fenway security has it out for me. Best behavior tonight. I decide to omit the story about Jen getting kicked out just a month ago. Ashley is not a beer drinker and we sweet-talk our way in the private club so she can have a liquor drink. As we quickly down our first round, I use one of my best tricks to get free drinks.

A Red Sox fan is intrigued with the *162* book, but not enough so to actually fork over $15. He asks if he can order it online. I get this a lot. They usually never do.

Watch what happens next.

I wink at Ashley and I take out a fresh *162* book and ask the Bostonian his name.

"Paul," he replies.

"Paul, I'd like to give you a complimentary copy of my book. A peace offering from a Yankees fan," I say with a smile and a handshake.

"Thanks!"

Wait for it ...

"Hey, what are you guys drinking?" he asks.

Bingo!

The law of reciprocity states that people like to repay things that are done for them. If one receives value, they like to return the favor as quickly as possible. It works again today as I have traded something that only costs me a few dollars and promotes my business and comedy. He proceeds to buy our next round. $22.

Paul knows that we were able to sneak into this club and encourages us to sneak into the Owner's Club.

"How do we get in?"

"Tell him that you are friends with the owner, John Henry," he says laughing, as we are fully decked out in Yankees garb.

My seat-jumping strategy isn't working as well tonight as we get kicked out of our seats several times. So, what do we have to lose? John Henry, here we come!

Ashley and I head for the Owner's Club. We approach the escalator where a young man with a walkie-talkie is stationed. He is the only person that we have to get past.

"Hey bud. We are here to see John Henry." I say confidently. "We just talked to his assistant, and she told us that we should come up. She said to call him if you need to."

He looks as confused as we seem confident. He stutters for a minute. "You don't have a club ticket?"

"No. But like I said, we just spoke with John's assistant. I tell you what, how about I go in and get her and bring her back?"

He looks puzzled.

"OK, but she has to wait here," he says pointing to Ashley.

I quickly scan his nametag. Ashley smiles and plays team. I take off and I'm in.

There are separate entrances to the individual private boxes, but I opt for the main bar area. I use some quick thinking and dial Danny.

"Hey, what's up?"

"Hey. I'm at Fenway. I don't have time to explain, but I'm trying to get in the owner's box and I need you to act like you are head of security. I need you to tell him to allow Ashley and I in. The kid's name is Jeremy."

He quickly agrees. I head back down and hand the kid my phone without saying anything.

Jeremy takes it and nods along, while listening intently. "

Yes, sir. OK. Will do. No, thank *you* sir."

Jeremy hands me the phone back and apologizes.

"Sorry guys. We don't get a lot of Yankees fans up here. Enjoy the rest of the game."

Boston strong!

It gets better. We nestle up to the bar and watch the rest of the game in style. We take advantage of the free drinks, some appetizers, and I line my pockets with cash as I make some *162* sales. I text Danny.

Nice work.

He instantly replies back.

Leave me out of your book. I have a pension.

Sorry big guy, it was too good of a story.

Monday, September 16

I awake with the knowledge that I have 15 games to go. I have yet to make a sign. Tonight is the night. I go through my head and try to come up with something creative.

How about *MOlicious*? That is so weak. *1 Mo to Go*? Sounds cool, but doesn't make sense (and I already used it in 2011). *Say it ain't so MO!* Maybe. But then it hits me: *Thanks for the MOmeries*. Hmm. I think I like it.

Ashley is there and is getting ready to leave for the airport. It's her birthday.

"Make sure the sign is bright yellow, so it sticks out," she advises.

I drop her off at Boston's Logan Airport and hit the local Wal-Mart to pick up everything from stencils to sharpies. It's go time. I'm back!

Mike picks me up at my hotel and we head for Fenway for the Sunday night game of the week and Boston's official Mariano sendoff. I have four tickets and we still need to scalp two. There is more supply than demand today. I've learned that the Sunday night games aren't as attractive to the locals, because the trains either stop running or on a very limited schedule.

I make my way to the streets. I don't want to deal with a scalper, but need to feel the vibe and see what tickets are selling for. The first guy offers me $20 for both.

"Really? You going to insult me like that? These are box seats."

"It's a rough night, I'm not trying to insult you."

"Really? Yankees vs. Red Sox and the Mariano farewell? Please!"

Another guy approaches and offers "$10 each."

"You are crazy. F--- you," I say and I walk away.

The crowd is there early for the ceremony as it is now close to 7 p.m.

I get my best offer of $30 each and turn it down.

"You won't get better than that," I'm told.

I make my way around yelling, "Who needs two box seats?"

I finally get the attention of a guy who is with his girlfriend.

"I have two really good seats," I tell them. He is hesitant and probably doesn't scalp often. Never say price first.

"I paid $100 each and I am right next to you," I reassure him. "They are great. I sat there yesterday."

The less you look like a scalper, the better. Scalpers don't go to the games.

"I was only looking to spend $50 each," he says.

I wince, which is another negotiating technique I have learned over the years.

"Ok, I can do that," I say with a touch of hesitancy as he hands over five twenties and I'm ready to go.

Mike and I sit in our seats as there is the usual buzz of a Yankees-Red Sox game. We are three rows off of the right field line and less than a first down to the bullpen.

At 7:40 p.m., the pre-game festivities begin. Ivan Nova throws his last warm up pitch and puts on his jacket. Towards the end of the National Anthem, a Yankees fan loudly screams, "Come on, Nova!" The Boston Symphony begins playing "Enter Sandman." It is a long song if you play it in its entirety. It seems even longer without Metallica singing the lyrics.

A Red Sox fan in the row behind me can't take the long intro. I heard him saying earlier that he was in town from Arizona. I'm not sure if he is on coke or always this obnoxious, but he loudly blurts out, "Enough already, Goddamn it!"

Oh, jeesh!

I'm usually pretty good at staying calm, especially at Fenway and try to obey my number one rule: Do Not Engage. Not tonight.

"Have a little respect, will ya?" I advise loud enough for everyone in our immediate section to hear.

He doesn't like my chastising and is taken back.

"Respect? How about that Yankee fan yelling during the National Anthem."

"So that guy's a dick. You have to be a bigger one? This is supposed to be a ceremony to honor Rivera. If you don't like it, come back when it is over."

We go back and forth as the other fans watch in anticipation. He reaches around and offers his hand. I shake it, but we still trade verbal jabs.

The PA announcer then continues the ceremony. "Tonight instead of toasting Mariano Rivera, we will begin by roasting him." Hmm. The Boston crowd roars with anticipation.

I am half pissed and half unsure of how to react. One of the most memorable games to Red Sox fans is game 4 of the 2004 ALCS. At the time Boston was down 3-0 in the series and had not won a championship in 86 years. Since 1918, to be exact.

A video introduces Kevin Millar. "Mariano was scared to pitch to me," he gloats.

The Fenway crowd starts to cheer.

They show the four-pitch at bat, in which Mo uncharacteristically doesn't even come close to the strike zone. I have mixed feelings as the Sox fans get louder with every pitch. Next they show former 2nd basemen Dave Roberts and how he entered the game to pinch run. What they don't say is what Rivera was going through that night.

Yankee fans will remember that Mo's cousin and his son were killed in a tragic accident a few days prior.

The cousin was like a brother and the incident happened in Mariano's home. They were taking care of Mariano's home during the season. The 14-year-old was electrocuted during a freak accident when a cable swung into the pool. Mo's cousin dove in the pool to save him and was electrocuted as well. Mo had missed game one and returned from the funeral in Panama during game two. Tough enough to deal with.

As Mo warmed up in the eighth inning, a Boston fan went way over the line. Just feet from the visitor bullpen, he loudly taunted Mariano about the death of his two relatives. Mariano explains the story in his book *The Closer*, but never once does he blame losing that game or the monumental collapse on that fan or anyone.

Interesting to know though, right? Again you never know what someone is experiencing. But his restraint and his classiness really shone through.

I remember Becki's words about why she respects Mo so much.

"He's a man of God and he's made having a relationship with God and being a Christian OK, and I appreciate that about him — both him and Andy Pettitte. Mo was given a talent, and he's used it without drama."

Speaking of drama, as I sit there with 37,000 Red Sox fans cheering along, I whisper to Mike, "Who is this a

The Last 42

tribute to? Mariano ... or the 2004 Red Sox?"

I guess this is a good representation of the relationship. The crowd gets rowdier as the huge video board replays Roberts stealing 2nd. A few excruciating minutes later, and after witnessing a recap of the 2004 World Series and the dramatic ALCS comeback, the scoreboard flashes, "But Seriously..."

And they go on to honor Mariano.

It doesn't take long for the beating to commence. The Red Sox score three in the first inning and the Yankees are never in this game. The sweep — and our playoff exit — seem inevitable.

At 9:25, an ESPN a commercial honoring Mo comes on and I am on the screen for three seconds.

"Everyone is going to miss him. He has been great for baseball," I say to the huddled masses that are watching. The texts start rolling in.

In the seventh inning, Mo makes his way to the bullpen. As Yankee fans know, he spends the first six or so in the dugout. The cheers begin as he makes what could be his final walk. I proudly hold up my newly-created sign. ESPN catches me doing so. Ashley texts me.

Just saw you on TV.

How'd I look?

Cute. Nice yellow sign :)

Mariano chats with the fans as he stands in the bullpen and watches on as a new Yankee warms up. As he sits on the bench, I am able to get his attention. I hold up my yellow sign and hold it for him to see. He smiles at me and waves. For two solid seconds Mariano Rivera and I have a moment. I nod my head and he nods back and mouths the words "thank you." Forty-two games in 45 days. It was worth it before, but now it is *really* cool.

The Red Sox expand their lead as Mike and I excuse ourselves from Fenway. This was my 15th game at Fenway. I hope to be back for the playoffs, but that is certainly looking bleak.

Visiting Boston was special this year and my heart goes out to the city and their residents that were attacked in April. I was glad I came to visit and see for myself how strong your resolve is.

Stay strong.

As we make our way down Yawkey, I run smack dab

into the security guard from a month earlier. We make eye contact as we continue to make our way briskly out of Fenway.

His look says, "I'm watching you."

Mine says, "You're a dick."

Chapter Thirteen

FLAT SCREENS IN HEAVEN

Wednesday, September 18

The mood is a little better tonight as the Yankees have broken a four-game slide. Down 3-0 in the 8th and with their backs against the wall, the Yankees finally fight back. After being held scoreless for 16 innings, NY scores four in the top of the 8th topped off by a Vernon Wells two-run double.

Mariano comes in during the 8th inning to relieve Robertson. With Brett Lawrie at the plate, Davis steals second base — his 42nd of the season — prompting Girardi to turn to Rivera and replace Robertson halfway through his at-bat. Three pitches later, the Yankees are in the dugout. Three out later and Mariano has saved his 44th of the year and his 652nd of his illustrious career. The Rogers Centre crowd of 24,247 rise to their feet to pay respects to the greatest closer of all time. We don't know it at the time, but we saw history tonight.

After the game, we return to the Loose Moose with the entire gang. My biggest priority is making sure that my cell phone has enough power for my 12:40 a.m. call from Sportsnet.

As I travel around promoting *162*, one of the most asked questions that I get is, "Have you met the Yankees?"

I always joke around that we hang in different circles. Quite frankly, it is expensive to just sit in their lobby's bar, if you are lucky enough to figure out where they are staying. In NY, there are so many options and they are virtually untouchable. On the road I am usually hanging out with local people who don't enjoy stalking adult ball players as much as I do.

My friend John Busch is visiting from Austin, Texas. He is staying at the very suave Thompson hotel. As soon as we walk in I am hit with a flashback from two years ago. I was in this fancy hotel on game 150 with my friend Chad from Australia. I recall a few memories from that day and fun night. That was the day that the Yankees interviewed me and subsequently the *162* story broke. This is a good sign.

We make it up to the room for a quick charge. There is a rooftop bar that we continue up to. The rooftop lounge has a 360-degree panoramic, unparalleled view. Simply amazing. *Chic* and *exclusive* are a few words that don't even begin to describe this 5-star hotel. I scope out a quiet location on the rooftop away from the buzz of the bar crowd for my post-game call.

Geri and John are seated on plush couches as we take in the sweeping views of Toronto's cityscape. John has been here a few days and has made friends with some of the wealthier guests. He introduces me to a gentleman who owns a chain of grocery stores in Ontario. The drinks are so expensive that I almost pass until I realize that the grocery mogul is treating. Geri and I get our order in as I turn to case the place out.

Just as Geri is raving about her $17 glass of wine, my head moves about 45 Degrees when I am slapped in the face with a challenge that I have been dreaming of since I can remember. It happens so quickly. I mumble something to Geri as I try to control my breathing. This is the moment that I have been waiting for.

Fifteen feet way, and standing all by himself, is Derek Jeter.

Oh jeeeeeeeesh!

Thank goodness I don't think about it for too long otherwise I may have talked myself out of it. Just as I approach The Captain, he begins to look at his phone.

Oh, no. Not this time, El Capitan. I can't tell if he was about to call someone or his phone is ringing, but I go for it.

"Hey Derek. I'm not sure if you know who I am or not, but I'm Steve Melia. The *162* guy."

He is very guarded, but trying to be respectful and is listening as his eyes appear to become wider. I'm guessing he hasn't heard of my record-breaking accomplishment or he is playing hard to get.

"In 2011, I attended every Yankee every game. All 162 and wrote a book about it."

His eyes widen a little more.

"Wait … *you're* Steve Melia?" he asks, clearly stunned. "Are you serious? Dude, I *love* your book! I actually bought a copy of it for all the guys on the team. And at Christmas, I ended up giving a bunch of them away as stocking stuffers to family and friends. This is incredible! I always wondered if I'd get the chance to meet you someday. Hey, you think I can get a picture with you?"

OK, that's not really the way it went down, but it's the way I *wish* it would have gone down!

In reality, Derek respectfully says, "It is nice to meet you," as he extends his right hand.

Hmm. I'm not sure is he heard me correctly. Sometimes I have to tell people twice and let it sink in. I am really nervous but continue.

"Yeah, I literally went to every game. Home and away. I met your dad in Cleveland."

Now I'm just trying to prolong the moment and think of something to say. Why did I mention his dad? That was weird.

"Well, I just wanted to introduce myself. It was great meeting you."

"Thank you. It was great meeting you, too."

I contemplate going to my book bag and pulling out a copy for him, but I'm sure that he doesn't want to carry it around all night and I don't want him to turn me down. I walk away and he gets swept away by a guy who seems to be escorting him around. It wasn't really the reception that a fanatic hopes for.

Maybe I made it awkward, and coupled with his protective shield around him, actually made it worse. I still did it, though. I am more proud of myself and appreciative of the universe for making it possible.

As I return to my circle I am immediately bombarded by other patrons, "Were you just talking to Derek Jeter?"

Yes. Yes I was. For that brief moment in time, of all the seven billion people on the planet, I, Steven McAuley

Melia, was chatting it up with Derek Sanderson Jeter. I look up at the sky and wonder if my brother Jim somehow arranged this little coincidence.

I now have a circle of bystanders that are hearing about my quest to do *The Last 42*. I sell two more copies as my lore begins to grow. At least *these* fans think I'm cool.

I laugh to myself as I reflect on meeting Jete. Like the song says, "I have been hanging out in all of the wrong places." They do not have rooftop lounges at the Comfort Inn. This could have been literally one of my last chances to talk to him while he is still playing. Tomorrow they leave right after the game. My last chance would have been in Houston.

My phone rings. It is the producer at 590 Sportsnet.

"Hey Steve. Welcome back to the show. You ready?"

I put the call on speakerphone as they are playing Metallica's "Enter Sandman." This is cool.

"There are fans of Mariano Rivera and then there are fans of Mariano Rivera," Jeff says as he sets up the 15-minute segment. It is a great interview. We talk about my brother Jim and why I was driven to accomplish this goal. He gives me some great plugs for the book. I talk about meeting Mariano and how we played pool for several hours. They even ask my opinion if the Yankees have a shot at the playoffs.

Just as we are finishing, a group is trying to make their way into our area. John stands up and is holding them off. He quietly mentions that I am being interviewed on sports radio. This seems to make them more interested in coming over.

As we hang up, the party of four walks over and introduce themselves. The lone female of the group is the most talkative and asks me about my book and my radio appearance.

"I have a lot of contacts in Vancouver," she says. "Have you been on the radio there?"

She then pulls out her wallet and buys a book. As I autograph it, one of her comrades with a big smile, interjects, "You should really get *her* autograph."

I learn that I am in the midst of five-time Olympian Charmaine Crooks. At one point she was the fastest woman in Canada and she is the first Canadian woman to run 800 meters in under two minutes. My new friend also won gold medals at the Pan American, Commonwealth, World Cup, and the World Student Games. Charmaine also took a silver in the 1984 Olympics.

She also turns out to be one of the nicest people. I pull out another book and this time I get *her* autograph.

We share with her our chance meeting with Derek Jeter moments ago. She said everything that Jeter would have said if we had more time, I'm sure.

"What you did is amazing. It is fans like you who make competing so worthwhile."

She made me feel really great and we all continued to socialize while looking over Lake Ontario. She is into big business now and is in town on a pretty big real estate deal. In addition to being a world-class athlete for several decades, Charmaine also has a gift of connecting with people. I'll treasure my meeting with her as much as I'll fondly remember finally meeting the Kid from Kalamazoo.

After they leave, we make our way down to the lobby bar, which offers a warm living room atmosphere. We walk in and the Yankees have multiplied. Jackpot! My old buddy, Derek Jeter, is seated on a coach comfortably next to CC Sabathia and Vernon Wells. There are a few more in their circle that I do not recognize.

I resist the temptation to just pull up a chair and sit with my boys. The bar is 20 feet past them. We pull up and I'm trying to nonchalantly point out the Yankees are in the house. Geri talks me into taking off my Bleacher Creature sweatshirt so I can proudly display my 162 jersey.

I gave CC Sabathia's parents two copies of my book back in June at the Oakland Coliseum. They were really jacked and promised to give CC his copy right after the game. There is a guy in LegalShield who went to high school with CC, and swore to me that CC knows who I am. He told me that they had an in-depth conversation about my tour.

These are the kind of thoughts swirling through my head like a hurricane as I see Jeter lean over to CC and point in my direction. I pretend to not be looking. He leans in closer to compensate for the loud music in the bar and appears to be explaining the 162 story.

Nice!

I fight the urge to go over and join their posse. I really feel like we bonded. Yeah, he was definitely talking about me. It probably went something like this,

"See that guy with the 162 Jersey? He is really cool. He said that he went to every game in 2011. Imagine that. What dedication."

Loose translation:

"See that psycho-looking guy over by the bar? I have a really uneasy feeling about him. If he starts coming over this way, watch his hands for weapons. I'll duck behind the couch. You clock him."

Either way, I finally got his attention.

Thirty-two games down and 10 to go.

Thursday, September 19

The beginning of the end. The last game in Toronto. I say this every night, but we really need to win the last 10.

Geri and I maneuver our way down to the front row behind the Yankees dugout. I even sell a few books to the Yankee fans in my vicinity. The Bombers are down 3-1 as we go to the bottom of the seventh. Kuroda has had enough. I am not at a loss of words as I see Joba Chamberlain jogging in from the right field bullpen. I yell my displeasure and question Girardi as he is only feet from me, securely in the visitor's dugout.

It seems like such a short time ago that I relished Chamberlain coming into a game. For a short time, he was the man who set up for The Man. Not anymore. Not even close.

Joba throws his first two pitches that aren't even close to the strike zone. I am losing it. I begin yelling.

"Take him out now, while we still have a chance!"

From my seat 350 feet away, I can tell we have a lefty and a righty ready to go in the bullpen. Chamberlain walks his 25th base runner of the year in just 47 innings. To everyone's surprise, Girardi leaves him in. Brett Lawrie runs the count to 3-1 before ripping a single. First and second no one out.

The lefty Adam Lind confidently walks up to the plate. I sit back and get ready for the inevitable pitching change. It only takes a split second to realize that Girardi is keeping him in. I pound on the visitor's dugout with my open palm.

CRACK! The ball explodes off the bat and disgust fills my body. Deep to right field. See ya. A three run homer for Adam Lind. 6-1 Toronto. *Now* Joe makes his way out to make a pitching change. A little bit too late. I'd say 14 pitches too late. I go from yelling to putting my hands in my face. You know when it is over. This sure seems like it.

Friday, September 20

It seems like I slept for five minutes. My alarm goes off at 4 a.m. No time for a shower today. I am already packed and move quickly out the door. I had a dream that seemed so real. I still can't believe that Girardi put Joba Chamberlain in when it mattered most, and even worse, left him in the game! Here's how my dream went:

With the Blue Jays leading the game 3-1 in the 7th and our playoff chances slimmer than an anorexic at a weight watchers meeting, Girardi goes to Joba.

I feel like I should do something. I am freaking out and banging on the dugout. "Take him out. Now!" I just can't believe what I am seeing. "Are you crazy, Joe? This guy's done. Now and forever." I feel so helpless. I wish that there is more that I could do.

Girardi is on the mound, but he is leaving Chamberlain in. Realizing that our only hope to save the season is a pitching change — now! With other Yankee fans booing around me, I decide to take action.

I slide onto the dugout roof and launch myself onto the field. As Girardi turns around I am jogging quickly towards him with my hands up in a questioning posture. I then use my arms like a crossing guard to stop the manager in his tracks.

"What are you doing? Our season is on the $%#@&*% line — and you are going to leave this guy in? He couldn't get an old lady out. Go to the lefty!"

Still in his path, I hold my left arm up and signal towards the right field bullpen by tapping on it with my right arm. I am signaling for Boone Logan.

"Boone is ready. You got 10 pitchers out there and you pick the one who can't get anyone out."

Michael Kay, the announcer, proclaims, "In all my years of broadcasting baseball, I can never remember a fan running on the field to argue with their own team's manager."

"Well, that fan has got a good point," conveys John Flaherty.

Derek Jeter, who is on the top step, leans in towards CC.

Flat Screens in Heaven

"That's the 162 guy ... that's who I was telling you about last night."

"Yeah, I see his jersey," CC replies. "I guess he's seen Joba one too many times."

Girardi keeps moving towards the dugout. As he approached the first base line, I take the opportunity to kick dirt in his direction.

Strangely, the umpires and security are frozen and just watch, like this is normal.

The scene goes to my brother's living room and Annie stoically announces, "Uncle Steve is on the field ... again. He's kicking dirt on Girardi."

"He better get not arrested again. He's only got nine games to go," Danny remarks with a smirk.

Becca looks up at the bar in the Dugout and screams, "Hey everyone, it's Steve Melia on TV at the game. He's going at it with Girardi!"

In a living room in Japan, a 10-year-old Japanese boy with big eyes, sits with his father and points.

"ご覧なさい１６２人の男がフィールドで口論しています。"
(Look! It's the 162 guy arguing on the field.)

His father points at the TV.

"わーっ、その男は狂信者です。 けれども彼は正しいで

251

す、Jobaは浮浪者で。" (Wow, that man is a fanatic; but he's right; Joba is a bum.)

The scene then shifts to heaven. My brother Jim is there with my parents and all of their siblings. He uses the remote to turn up the volume on the huge flat screen.

"Steve is on TV. He's gonna get thrown out of this game. Wait ... he's not even supposed to be in the game," Jim realizes.

"I told you, your brother is an idiot," my dad says holding up his scotch and toasting the television.

Everybody laughs. Fade to black.

My alarm goes off. My 100-minute nap is finished. So are the Yankees playoff chances because of Girardi and Chamberlain. Unbelievable. This is the most upset I have been at a managerial decision.

In Ontario, they have Smart Cars that can be rented for $10 an hour. Geri rarely needs a car but has an account and is kind enough to take me as the Subways aren't open at this hour.

It is a pretty cool service. She logs onto her computer and our Smart Car is just a few blocks away. We leave her place by 4:20 a.m. My flight is at 6:24. I'm not sure

Geri has a Smart solution to my transportation needs.

if it is the aerodynamics of this breadbox or three days of partying, (OK a month), but I have to roll down the window and get some fresh air, so I don't throw up going 55 mph. The Smart Car is tiny. I am really nauseous, but try to breathe through it.

Geri drops me off for my last nine games a few minutes before 5 a.m. The lines at the airport are unreal. I stand in line at the Delta counter for a solid 10 minutes. I hear an announcement that anyone with a 7 a.m. flight or earlier should move to the front. Hmm. I hustle to the front only to enter a separate room for customs with hundreds of people lined up in a never-ending maze. It is closing in on 5:30 now as I make my way to a security guard.

"Any chance that I can move to the front? My flight is at 6:24." He doesn't seem fazed. "Everyone is in the same boat, pal," he says with all the personality of a spoon.

I grab my spot and try to use all of my mind tricks to remain patient. There is a huge wall clock that I continually glance towards. 5:40 turns into 5:50 and eventually into 6 a.m.

At 6:10, I put my items on the conveyer belt and feel like I may still have a chance. The siren starts to go off and all lanes are stopped. There is a security breach and everything freezes. TSA just sort of stands around and waits for further instruction.

I remember the serenity prayer.

> *God grant me the serenity*
>
> *to accept the things I cannot change;*
>
> *courage to change the things I can;*
>
> *and wisdom to know the difference.*

A few minutes later, security is reopened and I sprint to my gate. It is one of those gates that seems like it is close, but the further I run the further it seems. There is no sign of activity as the door to the jet way is closed. The flight is gone. There is a couple in front of me in line who are doing all of the wrong things. Instead of taking responsibility for being late, they argue, show exasperation, and just act like overall jerks. The agent taking care of them continually tries to explain that they have missed their flight and the next available one isn't for seven hours into JFK. I take a different approach and try being nice.

"Sorry I am late. I am flexible as far as airports go, any chance that I could get a flight into LaGuardia instead of JFK?"

The agent appreciates my laid back demeanor and somehow gets me on a different airline. She whispers so the other passengers won't hear, "I'm really not supposed to do this, but I got you on a 9:30 into LaGuardia on West Jet." I return the kindness by autographing her a *162* book.

I have a few hours to kill but am totally exhausted. I walk up to my new gate and am greeted with a huge smile from the West Jet agent. She hooks me up with a business class seat for simply being nice. I ask her if she likes to read as I take out my last book.

"Thank you so much," she says. "I am flying to Europe tonight and I need something to read."

I always find it strange when people are sprawled out and sleep over three or four seats in an airport terminal. With a few hours to kill and no desire to sit in the airport bar and begin sipping on overpriced drinks, I make my way to an area that looks uninhibited.

I take off my Bleacher Creature sweatshirt and use it as a pillow. An hour later, I awake to the same dream of me storming the mound to remove Joba. "Should have taken him out," I mumble to myself as I wipe off some drool and notice other passengers looking at me with a hint of disdain.

Maureen and Danny are both working today and I will need to take public transportation. I arrive at LaGuardia and jump on a bus that delivers me to Jamaica station and the Long Island Railroad. I miss my train by seconds and wait 30 minutes for the next one.

Maureen picks me up at the Rockville Centre station and nine hours after waking up, I walk into the house totally run down. No rest for the fanatics.

I awake 30 minutes later from power nap to learn that Andy Pettitte is holding a press conference today at 3 p.m. He is announcing his retirement. I leave for Yankee Stadium and turn on the Michael Kay show to listen live.

For months the talk has been of Mariano and unfortunately of A-Rod. Today talk radio switches to focus on Pettitte. He has been an important part of a dynasty for a decade and a half and has more wins than anyone in postseason history.

The consensus is on sports radio that he won't make the Hall of Fame. He was good, even great at times, he just doesn't have the dominant Hall of Fame numbers. Andy will pitch on Sunday, so Yankee Stadium will get to say goodbye. Sunday will be amazing. I was able to attend Jorge Posada's entire last season and now I get to watch his friends close it out.

I have been waiting for the call from Ed Randall who hosts a show on WFAN in NY called "Talking Baseball." He heard about *The Last 42* and has invited me to be on his show. I look down to see that I have received a call from 917 and I have a voicemail. I listen right away.

"Steve, its Ed Randall, and its almost 9:00 on Friday. I'm going to do everything I can to have you on tomorrow. It's been a heavy news day with the announcement that Pettitte will be packing it in., but I'll do everything I can. If I can still get you on it will be tomorrow after the game in the latter stages of the show. I'll have to call you tomorrow; I have a lot going on. Talk to you later."

I can hear background noise so I know that he is at the stadium as well.

In the bottom of the seventh, the bases are loaded and in steps A-Rod. I am along the third base line in a pretty good seat. These are the high-priced mostly corporate seats and usually the fans in this section are pretty mel-low. But one Yankees fan who has apparently enjoyed one too many adult beverages is now standing yelling at the top of his lungs.

"You suck A-Rod. You suck. You are a bum. You suck!"

This guy is annoying everyone else in the section. With the count 1-1, a medium-sized Yankee fan of about 50 walks right up to the other so-called fan.

"You know who sucks? *You* suck!" he blasts at the top of his lungs. Everyone cheers as the loudmouth quickly shuts up and sits down. You gotta love New York. A-Rod has come a long way in a month; Yankee fans are actually sticking up for him!

A split second later, Alex rips an opposite field bomb that lands just over Becki's head in right field. Alex's fan is bombarded with high fives and fist pumps. So is Alex, by his teammates. I get a text from my brother Dan.

A-Rod just broke Lou Gehrig's record for grand slams.

He now is the all-time leader with 24. 5-1 Yankees.

The Yankees win the next two games pretty easily and the victories could not have come at a better time. They are still three games behind the Indians, who beat the Astros, in the chase for the second AL Wild Card with just eight games to play. But New York leapfrogged the Orioles and Royals, who both lost Saturday, and they're now behind the Texas Rangers who are a half-game back for the second Wild Card.

Book sales have been up over the Yankees last home stand. It is good that I listened to Bald Vinny and didn't quit after the first few days. When the Yankees win, people buy. The fans are in a good mood with the big sendoff tomorrow and our postseason hopes are still alive.

I look down at my phone to see that I have a missed call from the 212 area code. No message, though. I dial the number and I am put on hold by CBS Sports The Fan 660. The Fan was the first 24-hour sports radio network in the world. Yikes, I missed the call! I quickly call Ed Randall on his cell.

He asks if I'm ready. They will call me back. I turn to George as customers are just lingering on this gorgeous day in Da Bronx and ask him to watch my stuff as I am about to be interviewed on the radio. As usual, he agrees and I scurry away to the park across the street — which is where the old Yankee Stadium was located — to get away from the loud train that passes by every three or four minutes. I wait patiently as I try to find the perfect location. Being on the radio in other cities is fun, but there is nothing like the limelight in New York.

I text my brothers and tell them to tune into 660 AM. Here are some excerpts from the interview.

ER: We have heard amazing stories over the past few weeks about what teams, players, and fans are doing to honor Mariano. Wait until you hear what our next guest is doing. He is attending every one of Mariano Rivera's last 42 games of his career. Steve Melia welcome to "Talking Baseball."

SM: Thanks, Ed, for having me on the show.

ER: Steve, tell us what you are doing and what inspired you.

SM: I wrote a book about my last experience of attending all 162 games in 2011. I was on the road in Nashville, TN, marketing the book and I got some really bad news. Just over a month ago we learned that one of my brothers passed suddenly of a heart attack at 47.

ER: I'm so sorry.

SM: Yeah, thank you, Ed. I come from a family of firefighters. My dad was a deputy chief here in the city. Two of my brothers, also. Dan Melia is a chief now and my brother Tommy retired a few years ago. I grew up here in NY and moved when I was 8. I just wanted to do something to remember my brother Jim, but also to honor Mariano. I would watch the road games on TV as the other teams honored Mo and would think how awesome it would be to be there in person. When my brother passed, I said I'm gonna do it. The idea just popped into my head. The Last 42. So I decided to just do it. I've been to the last 35 games. Seven to go and — who knows — we *might even just have a shot at the playoffs here.*

ER: *Steve, what is it about this guy that has captured your heart?*

SM: *I think it was 2005, Ed, I had the great fortune of walking into a hotel lobby bar out in California, where I was living. I was with my wife at the time, Kim, my brother Mike, and my nephew Willie and playing pool was Mariano Rivera. There was no one else around. No fanfare. Just...*

ER: *Wait just a minute. Wait — back up, back up. Tell us how you got how him to play pool?*

SM: *We walked in the bar and he was the only Yankee there. He literally invited us to play. He was racking the balls and he looked up and in his beautiful accent, asked, " Does anyone want to play with me?" I raised my hand like a first grader. I was like, "I would like to play." We played for two hours. We actually beat him the first two games because his partner scratched on the 8 ball. In all my time of ever playing pool, he was the best player I have ever played with.*

ER: *Really?*

SM: *Yes. He really was. Everything he does is so intentional. His focus, the spin on the ball. Another thing that I'll always remember was his attitude. He had a great attitude, but he did not like to lose to us. We beat him the first two games and then he beat us three games in a row.*

ER: *(laughing)* But when you are up two games to nothing, did you feel badly for him or anything?

SM: No, not at all. I was actually taunting him. I was like, "The Melias are beating the greatest closer of all-time." He was laughing and having fun. He had a great attitude. He was so engaging. He was everything that you hope that someone you really idolize would be. He was not pretentious by any means. He was funny. He listened. He called us by our first names — although he kept calling me James for some reason. Kim, Mike, and Willie still kid me about that. It was such a great experience getting to know the person, Mariano Rivera. I never heard anyone ever say anything ill-willed about him. For me this was amazing to help him close out his career this way.

ER: Wow. You hear so many stories from people that have met him about what a nice person this is. We can add one more to the list ... Steve Melia has, since August the 16th, been stalking in the most friendly way possible, Mariano Rivera, both home and away. He's giving new meaning to the term stalking. Starting in Fenway Park, just to be present for the games that the greatest closer of all time might appear in. In 2011, many of you remember that Steve attended all the Yankees home and away games. Steve, safe travels, and congratulations on this. I think that it's wonderful.

The New York sports world has just officially heard about *The Last 42*. This was a great day.

Later that night I pull into my brother Tommy's house. It is surreal to be back to the house that was my base for the 2011 season. Tommy is going with me to the farewell and it will be easier to crash at his place.

Chapter Fourteen

THE TIPPING POINT

Sunday, September 22

There have been very many special games played at the Polo Grounds, the old, and now the new Yankee Stadium. Today we will honor two men who wore the pinstripes proudly and often.

I make it to the kitchen table, the scene of many *162* morning chats. Tommy looks up from the *Daily News*.

"You going to the game today?"

"I was thinking about it."

We both smile as this was how he greeted me almost every morning for 81 home games over six months in the summer of 2011.

We jump on his computer to download our tickets.

Tommy's eyes are as big as softballs as he sees that I paid $270 for two bleacher seats. I was going to treat him, but he insists on paying his own way to see a little bit of history today. There is a buzz in the air. Every Creature is in the house today.

We pull into the Bronx at 10:30 a.m. My first customer is waiting on me as I drop my table and books off in front of Billy's Sports Bar.

"Were you on The FAN yesterday?"

"That was me."

"Well, that was a great interview. A really cool story."

He didn't say it, but I suspect that he lost someone close to him, maybe even a brother. I can tell by the warmth in his smile and empathy in his eyes. As he is walking away, the same scenario plays out. The difference between today and tomorrow is that fans are coming with their money out already.

"I'll take one," says the next guy in line.

"How'd you hear about the book?"

"Ed Randall, yesterday on The Fan. Talking Baseball. I love that guy."

"Me too. He was really cool."

My first customer is hovering and reaches back in and

says, "You are going to do really well today."

I smile back as I look over to see a line starting to form.

There's a commonly used phrase called "the tipping point." It pertains to a lot of different areas of life when an event happens and everything changes. In sales, this happens when a product, service, or idea goes from being sold to being *bought*. I think about this as I frivolously sign two more copies for my next customer.

Tommy comes back from the Court Deli with an egg sandwich, my first thing to eat for the day. He can't believe the difference a few weeks makes as he starts to talk to a few potential customers.

All of the cool Yankee fans I have met in the last six weeks stop by Bald Vinny's House of Tees. Becki has her dad with her today as she introduces him around. I can tell that he is having a great time with his daughter. I sign his book and inscribe, "Live <u>Your</u> Dreams! You have an amazing daughter that you should be proud of!"

Udi shows up and discusses everything from our potential playoff chances to next season's schedule. Bald Vinny and George have a huge crowd around them as well and everyone is picking up their favorite Bleacher Creature shirts. Business is booming!

It is hard to tear away as this is my best day of selling books. At 11:50 with a few dozen sold, I begin to pack up. Bald Vinny comes over.

"Where are you going?"

"We don't want to miss the ceremony."

I can tell that he doesn't buy that as he looks at his watch.

"OK," I admit. "We are going to hit The Dugout for a few quick beers."

He laughs and we are off.

The papers said to be in our seats at 12:15 and that is what we plan to do. We make our way into my favorite bar in the Bronx and notice that no one is drinking. Becca smiles and points at her watch and holds up the number three. I look at my phone. 11:57. Hmm. They do not serve until noon. We decide to go in.

I think to myself how lucky I am to witness this "Mo"mentous occasion. My brother Tommy and I cheer with the other 50,000 lucky fans as all of our modern-day Clipper heroes are introduced one by one.

We are seated in 202, one section away from the Bleacher Creatures. We are directly under the George Steinbrenner mural. Tommy and I snap a picture with The Boss before the section becomes too packed. It is too crowded today to sneak over and try to meld in with The Creatures. I really wanted to hang out with them today

The Tipping Point

as I am growing fonder of them each game.

So we sit and stand in the very packed bleachers. Tommy has a pretty big guy pressed against him who has a very bad skin condition and is sweating like crazy. The enthusiastic lady next to me keeps standing on the bench in front of us as her long flowing hair keeps finding its way into my $12 beer.

In front of us is a guy of about 50 with his elderly mother. Before the ceremony starts, he is constantly watching after her and helps her put two more layers of clothing on. She must be around 80. It is very sweet and touching to see as it reminds me of our mom and how fragile life can be. The smallest of things tend to make me emotional since August 2nd.

At some point the child becomes the caregiver. The tipping point. Watching this macho guy being so tender makes my eyes tear up. On this tour and in remembrance of my brother Jim, I continue to attempt to ap-

The Last 42

preciate the little things and not be so quick to be exasperated or annoyed by outside influences.

For the last five weeks I have been in the middle of Mo hysteria. What did I learn that maybe I didn't already know? I think more than anything I confirmed what I already knew: The man that Mo is and the heart that he has is appreciated by every single person that I run across. Everyone loves and appreciates the way that he treated them. That is Mo. He's genuine. He cares. He's patient when he talks to people. He's also very positive and encouraging. He makes other people feel important. He remembers where he came from. And he has certainly come a long way from a fishing boat in Panama.

His first flight at age 20 was to spring training and he did not speak one word of English. To this day, he has kept his promise to Tim Cooper not to "big-league" anyone. His faith in God has kept him humble.

The ceremonies begin with John Sterling, voice of the Yankees Radio, and Michael Kay, the voice of YES Network. Both of these guys have announced for Mo his entire career. Sterling was at every one of his games. The part that I am looking forward to the most are the introductions of the former Yankee greats who played with Mo.

John Wetteland, Tino Martinez, Bernie Williams, Paul O'Neill, Hideki Matsui, Jeff Nelson, David Cone, and

Jorge Posada are all introduced to huge ovations. Gene Monahan, longtime friend and Yankees trainer, makes his return to honor Mo. Representing MLB is Mariano's former manager, Joe Torre. You know it's a good party when Torre shows up.

Jackie Robinson's family is escorted out to the diamond by Jackie's namesake, Robinson Cano. The Yankees unveil a statue in Monument Park of Jackie Robinson. Mo's wife, Clara, and their three sons are walked out by Yankee captain, Derek Jeter.

At many points the crowd breaks out into the familiar chant:

MAH-REE-AHH-NOOOO.

MAH-REE-AHH-NOOOO.

MAH-REE-AHH-NOOOO.

It is reminiscent of July 9th, 2013, when Derek Jeter hit number 3,000. Just as loud. Just as emotional.

The cameras switch to Monument Park where Mo is with his family. For the first time ever, a player's number is retired while he is still wearing it.

The last 42.

They unveil the plaque and he is right next to Ron Guidry's # 49. Mayor Michael Bloomberg declares it Mariano Rivera day. Metallica takes the stage in center field, the bullpen door swings open, and the man of honor begins his journey in for one of the last times. Only he doesn't trot. He walks. He seems to be really embracing his retirement party with his big smile.

The ceremony continues on for nearly an hour as fans, teammates, and baseball dignitaries express their appreciation and admiration. Our section is so packed that after the ceremony we make our way to much better seats. We are going to take this one in in style. The best seats never fill up because the mega rich don't care as much.

During every half inning, the Jumbotron features star after star recognizing Mariano. The messages are so similar that it seems like the Yankees prompted them in what to say.

Every person, and there are many, say that it was honor to know him and how they watched how he handled himself on the field and off the field. Over and over. What a testament.

There are stars from other sports such as Charles Barkley, Patrick Ewing, Victor Cruz, Eli Manning, and Mark Sanchez. The crowd cheers when former teammates like Nick Swisher and Jason Giambi pop up on the Jumbotron. TV stars like Kelly Rippa and Michael Strahan represent the entertainment field.

Although it is a special day, we need to win this game.

Pettitte is as good as I have ever seen him. He retires the first 14 batters as Tommy and I watch from Section 125 down the third base line.

A Mark Reynolds homerun gives us a 1-0 lead in the third. In the fifth, Andy allows the first base runner by giving up a walk. Andy is moving along nicely. Amazing, really.

In the top of the sixth, the storybook ending takes a wrong turn as Ehire Adrianza hits his first Major League homer. The Yankees threaten in the 6th and 7th, but can't get anyone across the plate and leave two men stranded in both frames. We continually glance up at the scoreboard to see that Cleveland and Tampa are both winning. A loss will put us four games out with six to go.

Andy begins the 8th having thrown 102 pitches. Pablo Sandoval chases the 41-year-old left-hander with a double to left field, which is just the second hit that Pettitte has allowed.

That will be the final pitch Pettitte will throw wearing the illustrious Yankees pinstripes.

Joe Girardi makes his way out to the mound as the Stadium crowd slowly rises to their feet. Pettitte slams his glove against his thigh and awaits his manager and former catcher. Andy gives him the ball and the Yankee Stadium crowd gets to thank Number 46 for an incredible career. Like his friend Mo, he did it with class.

He makes his way to the dugout as the crowd simultaneously chants, "An-dy Pet-titte, An-dy Pet-titte."

Derek Jeter is the first to embrace him as he waits on the top step. The crowd continues as Andy makes his way through the dugout and gets hugs from his teammates and he returns for one more curtain call. Today he gave us what we needed. He was a total stud. Seven innings, one walk, and two hits. Vintage Pettitte. Like he was so many times before, Andy was dandy.

Our future closer comes running out of the bullpen attempting to save the season. David Robertson has been shaky lately compared to his last two years in the 8th inning role. But the baton has been passed. It's his time now. The tipping point.

He quickly retires the first batter as the lead runner moves to third. His first pitch to Tony Abreu is a double to right sending the go-ahead run scrambling to the plate.

"I feel like I let everybody down," Robertson said afterwards. "I let Andy down."

The bullpen doors swing open for Mariano Rivera, a non-save situation for the all-time saves leader. An important one, though. The fans seem not to care what the score or situation is as we stand and cheer the man who helped bring five rings to New York.

Mo blows away Ehire Adrianza on three strikes. He gets the last out on a fly ball to Granderson in center.

Everyone is wondering the same question: Is the magic alive in the Bronx? A-Rod leads off with a single and is replaced by pinch runner and rookie Zoilo Almonte. Robbie Cano hits a double as Almonte stops at third and the Bombers are in business. Second and third with no outs.

Alfonso Soriano steps up. Without Soriano's return to the Bronx, we wouldn't even be in the hunt still. He grounds it to third as Almonte hesitates briefly before breaking for home. Third baseman Noonan fields it and fires home for the first out. When Almonte briefly froze, Cano felt forced to stayed on second. Hmm.

First and second with one out. Curtis Granderson fails to deliver or even move the runners and strikes out. The rollercoaster of emotion is sweeping through Yankee Stadium.

Eduardo Nunez slaps a hard single through the left side. The magic is briefly alive. Juan Perez, the left fielder, fires it in just ahead of Robinson Cano. Catcher Hector Sanchez, fields it cleanly and makes the tag for the third out.

Two players tagged out at home to preserve the lead for the defending World Series champs. We are running out of chances. Mariano comes in and protects the lead in the ninth. The lineup in the bottom half of the ninth looks pitiful and is, unfortunately, a glance into the future.

Due up is Mark Reynolds, Brendan Ryan, and JR Murphy. There is no one else left on the bench to pinch hit. Many of the readers are probably googling these names. One of the biggest days at the new stadium ends anti-climatically as the Yankees go down in order. Reality is setting in.

Monday, September 23

The Yankees are four behind Cleveland and 4½ behind Tampa. Maureen and I sit at the kitchen table.

"How bad is it? Do we still have a chance?"

"Slim at best," is my grim response.

My two hours of PR work in Toronto really paid off as I landed both radio interviews as a result. I also heard back from Marty Appel, former PR Director with the Yankees. Marty thought *162* was very cool and remarked that we would be forever linked in the libraries of books. He wrote a book called *162-0*. This is a book that highlights the 162 best NY Yankee wins ever.

Today is my last off-day, barring a miracle playoff appearance. I have to mail out about 10 books to various people including Marty and a few others. I was holding off booking my return trip from Houston, thinking that I would need to fly somewhere for the Wild Card game. With reality setting in, I start looking at my last flight of *The Last 42*.

I consider asking the Yankees for a ride on their jet. Yeah — probably not. I've emailed them three times and haven't heard anything from their media director, Jason Zillo. In his defense, he has a pretty intense time with Andy Pettitte retiring as well. He has been working 24/7 getting ready for the farewell.

Tuesday, September 24

Six games to go. The Yankees chances are getting slimmer. Tampa, KC, and Texas all won last night, putting us on the brink of elimination.

I get a Facebook message from Jimmy Jenkins from Virginia, whom I met through Bald Vinny. Jimmy ordered a *162* book a few months back and claims to have loved it. He is in town for Mo's final game this Thursday. Last night he asked how I am for the Houston series. I told him that I was good except for Sunday. Within an hour he had emailed three field-level seats for Mariano's last game and my last game of *The Last 42* tour.

One might feel funny that people you don't even know are spending money on you. I have come to learn that people like to do nice things. It makes them feel better. I appreciate it just the same, though. Jimmy Jenkins is the official sponsor for game 162, or the last of my 42. Jimmy Jenkins, this Bud's for you!

Tonight it is Mariano Rivera bobblehead night. I personally am not a big fan of the giveaway promotions. It just serves as distraction to what we should be paying attention to ... the actual game. With only three home games and us hanging on to the playoffs like a frayed piece of dental floss, let's confuse the issue and give away a doll.

First sign of a problem. They are only giving them away to the first 18,000 fans.

Tonight I have several good friends coming to the game. Slug, my college roommate, is coming with his dad. His main mission is to get a Mariano bobblehead. His main challenge is that he is always late.

My friend The Breeze is also joining the party with his new girlfriend. The Breeze looks like he's straight out of Duck Dynasty with a full red beard and ball cap.

Maureen, Annie, and Katie are coming as well. I will not be sitting with any of them.

Maureen drives in with me. We pull into the Bronx and are set up at Bald Vinny's House of Tees by 4:45. The line outside of the stadium is unlike any I have never seen. The huge area in front of the stadium is at a standstill. There are people everywhere. A mob scene.

I overhear Bald Vinny talking on his cell. "It's gonna be a nightmare. The bobbleheads aren't even here yet." We won't find this out until later, but the truck carrying the dolls has broken down in NJ.

He hangs up and looks at me and George. "This is going to be a fun night."

Although there are 20K-plus Yankees fans just hundreds of feet away right across the street, business is slow for us as no one wants to leave their spot in line to buy anything.

The gates usually open at 5 p.m. Not tonight. The crowd continues to grow, as the mob scene is spilling over into the streets. In the world of social media, word begins to spread and the early birds are getting restless.

Right before 6 p.m., the gates finally open and the first 18,000 fans (or so) receive a *voucher* for a Mariano Rivera bobblehead. I guess they have decided to deal with the problem later. I ditch my plan to close up early and grab my own souvenir.

Maureen and the girls go in, but they are out of vouchers by the time get they get through the line. Slug stops by my booth as does The Breeze. Becki shows up and hands me my ticket. This is probably the last time we will get to hang out for a while.

We must win tonight to be able to pull off a miracle. Hiroki Kuroda's third pitch of the game to Matt Joyce is launched into the right field seat about 30 feet to our left. With a W-L record of 15-4, that is all Tampa's Matt Moore is going to need. The Rays push across two more and never look back.

In the third inning, the fiasco worsens as the PA address announcer declares, "Attention fans. Those fans who received vouchers may now pick up their Mariano Rivera bobblehead at Gate 2."

Fascinating. I would have thought they would have bitten the bullet and shipped the dolls to those with vouchers. Nope. They decide to make the fans wait in line ... yet again. Many of these fans, mostly families with small children, have been in Da Bronx since 4 p.m. They waited in line for two hours and now they are back for Round 2.

Between our non-existent offense, stellar Devil Ray's pitching, and the bobblehead-ache, the fans are not even a factor.

I witness fans of all ages sprinting down the stairs headed for Gate 2. With the Yankees on the brink of elimination, a very large percentage of the stadium gets up at the same time to get in line. Throughout the night, the line continues to grow and doesn't seem to be moving at all. Many fans are cutting in line only compounding the animosity and frustration. I'm glad that I'm not into promotions.

I make my way past thousands of fans who have now been in line for 90 minutes. The line wraps around the entire stadium and goes onto the second level. They look worn out. Many probably figure that they have come this far and can't turn back now. The tipping point.

We use my ticket trick to get into my normal seats directly behind the Legacy section. What I witness next only adds to the Yankee's PR nightmare.

A stadium employee is walking around with a large box, in full view of the entire Yankee Stadium crowd, handing out bobbleheads to everyone in that section. Now, I'm pretty confident that none of these people were part of the first 18,000 fans. The rich get richer.

Our not-so-magic number is one. One loss or a win by Tampa, Texas or KC, and we are eliminated.

Wednesday, September 25

In the papers this morning, Yankees Media Relations guy, Jason Zillo, defends the organization by saying that the Yankees handled the situation as good as to be expected. Right. Sports radio is all over the snafu as well. Try again, Jason.

Halfway through the day, the Yankees announce that anyone with a ticket from last night will be comped to a game in 2014 to make up for any inconvenience. A nice gesture but, I believe that anyone with a ticket stub should receive the Mo doll in the mail.

There are many rituals in Section 203. I am only beginning to learn all of the nuances. One thing I know for sure: "The Wave" never makes it to 203.

I have always seen The Wave as merely a distraction. It does bother me when there is a big moment in the game and the fans couldn't care less and are more worried about all standing in unison like some weird game of human dominoes.

I always had an inclination to not like The Wave. Now, because of my newly-found affiliation with The Creatures, I despise The Wave. It certainly is easier to form an opinion when you are part of a fanatical group.

Many claim to have started The Wave, but none more passionately than Oakland A's fanatic, 68-year-old Krazy George. "I don't *claim* I invented The Wave. I *did* invent The Wave," he says modestly.

The first recorded Wave occurred in Oakland at an Athletics' playoff game against the New York Yankees on Oct. 15, 1981.

Krazy George Henderson planted The Wave wherever he went after that A's game in 1981. But George says The Wave didn't suddenly spring up out of thin air that October day in Oakland.

"Wave" to the camera, Krazy George!

"It took me three years of different forms and modifying it and changing and evolving till it got to the Oakland A's game," he says. And, actually, when he explains it, the seeds were planted more than a decade before when he was a cheerleader at San Jose State.

According to ESPN, in 1970, George did a section cheer for the student body that involved one section standing up and yelling "San," the next standing and yelling "Jose" and a third doing the same thing with "State."

"It looked dynamic to see these three full sections go San ... Jose ... State," he says. "And it would go five or six times in a row ... That cheer was like the nucleus at the start of the idea of a Wave type of idea."

By the time it got to Oakland, the wave was fully developed and it was only a matter of time before the entire sports world embraced it. The tipping point.

But not in Section 203, Krazy George. Not tonight at Yankee Stadium. Tonight, we will honor our Superfan Bald Vinny on his birthday by remaining seated. Vinny and George are handing out "Ban The Wave" buttons as a reverse birthday present.

Many people are coming bearing gifts to their favorite Superfan. Over the last three seasons, I have learned that Vinny has a gift himself. He is great with people. Like most successful people I have ever met, he has the knack of making other people feel important and included.

I wait for a rare quiet moment when no else is around. "Hey Vin, I got you a little present."

I hand him my commemorative coin from FDNY's 10-year anniversary of 9/11.

"I got this at the FDNY celebrity breakfast in remembrance of 9/11."

"No way!" he exclaims with big eyes. "I totally collect stuff like this." He gives it a good look and turns it over. "Man this is really cool. I am putting this on my mantle."

Joining me at the game is a friend from LegalShield,

Wayne Stevens, who scored us great seats from his boss, Mike. Two weeks prior, Mike stopped by the table and picked up a copy of *162*. Tonight he sponsors "Ban The Wave" night.

Also joining us is my nephew, David McElwee. David made his primetime debut on HBO, less than 72 hours prior, with a speaking part on *Boardwalk Empire*. Dave, 25, has been acting since I can remember. He has paid his dues to his craft and it is starting to get paid back in dividends with fame.

He grew up in Florida and graduated from Florida State majoring in Theater. This is where his Uncle Jim went to college as well. After a stint in LA, he now lives in Brooklyn and is aggressively pursuing his acting career. I admire his "all-in" attitude. Jim lived with the McElwee clan as he began his stint as an underpaid teacher. He was always proud of Dave.

"Welcome to Da Bronx," I greet my nephew. "How does it feel?" He knows that I am referring to his newly-found celebrity status.

"The last 48 hours have been amazing. I am hearing from people that I forgot I knew," he says.

"You were really good. People love that show, too. You made it." We exchange a man hug and a fist bump.

Watching someone close to you going for it and living out a dream is so inspiring. I've been watching this kid since he was born. His mom, Eileen, is my sister and godmother and I know how proud he has made both of his parents.

He seems almost as equally impressed with my makeshift bookstore. We haven't seen each other since the day of the funeral and we have the "How-have-you-been-holding-up" conversation. Dave helped run the memorial service since he was a staple in the Cocoa Beach theater community.

Officer Wayne Townsend makes his daily stroll up River Ave. I am now in the half-bear-hug group as he comes over to say his daily hellos.

"Wayne this is my nephew, David," I proudly announce.

One of the NYPD's finest and friendliest cops reaches out his hand.

"You look familiar. You're not wanted, are you?" he asks, cracking himself up.

I jump in to brag on my godson. "You ever watch *Boardwalk Empire*?"

That was all I needed to say and all that I was *able* to say for the next 20 minutes.

It was like the rest of the world didn't exist for Townsend. He takes a step forward and declares, "I *knew* I recognized you! I've never missed an episode. Were you on this week? What character are you?"

"Yes, on Sunday," David said. "I played Roger's friend, in the restaurant scene."

The officer's eyes light up. "Wow. *Boardwalk* is my favorite show! This is amazing."

His walkie-talkie goes off as he half-heartedly listens in, but continues his conversation.

"So you got to work with Ron Livingston. He was in *Office Space*, right? How about Steve Buscemi?"

Dave is having fun and seems to have a new best friend. After Jim's death I strive to appreciate every moment. I stand back and think about all of the tireless work, obstacles overcome, and thousands of hours that Dave has put in to get to this point. One minute you're a starving artist doing community theater, and the next minute you're getting recognized by people everywhere for your work on one of the hottest shows on television. The tipping point.

Townsend comes over with his camera and hands it to me, "Let's get a picture. This kid is going to be famous."

I try to finagle my way in, but the NYPD officer is content with a pic of just him and Dave.

"I gotta go fight crime, boys. It was great meeting you," he says as he walks away with a huge smile. He turns back to Dave one more time.

"You are going to be a big star. I can feel it." He holds his phone up like a prize he won at the state fair, "And I'll have a picture to prove that I knew you when!"

My nephew and I agree — that was pretty cool.

We meet my friend Wayne and I pack it in a little early as we make our way over to The Dugout. It is packed in the bar as I spot Motorcycle Pete. The nearest corner of the bar on the right is like his second home. Pete and I have been texting since we met and I consider meeting him to be one of the highlights of the tour.

When I did *162*, it was like I was by myself. On *The Last 42* tour, I feel like I have a lot more friends.

"Did you see the *NY Post* today?" He signals to Becca, behind the bar to hand him the paper. "Check this out."

There is a picture of him, a guy named Jamal, and a beautiful young woman named Nicole. In the picture they are holding up Nicole as she is next to the street sign on 161st and River Ave. She is holding a makeshift sign that says *Rivera* Ave. Nicole is a woman on a mission. She wants *River* Ave. to one day be *Rivera* Ave. She says that she will stop at nothing. It's funny to watch how passionate she is.

She is browsing through *162* and stops on page 185. She reads about me jumping on Shea Stadium's field.

After reading silently, she stops to ask, " Will they really fine you $5,000 for running on the field? I'm glad I read this, I was thinking of streaking tonight."

Oh, jeesh.

Jamal and I talk at the bar. I learn that he hasn't missed a home game since July of 2009 when he attended his father's funeral — 275 games or so. The amazing part is that he is a full-time high school teacher.

"How do you go to the day games?"

Day games are at 1 p.m. and there are usually a dozen or so every year. A huge smile slides across his face.

"I schedule all my classes in the morning. I duck out of my planning period when I need to. Everyone at that school knows that I go to all of the Yankees games."

He sounds more like a college student than a teacher. We share a few beers before going in to watch the 2013 NY Yankees officially get eliminated from the postseason.

From the elation of competing in the playoffs 16 of the last 17 seasons to the disappointment of having to watch it from home on TV.

The tipping point.

Chapter Fifteen

THERE *IS* CRYING IN BASEBALL

Thursday, September 26

I get to Da Bronx for the last time in 2013. This is the first meaningless game ever that I've ever been to at Yankee Stadium. Meaningless in the fact that the Yankees are out of postseason contention. But don't tell Yankee fans this game is meaningless, because it is far from that.

The pressure is off. The excitement is on. River Ave. has a buzz. I get a text from Motorcycle Pete.

Make sure you come to The Dugout. We have to get a picture with my motorcycle.

I pull up and like he does everyday, George greets me with a fist pump. Over the last six weeks, we have become buddies. I like George and I enjoy our new daily rituals.

He is with Chris Gager, who is headed back to Kentucky after the game. Chris has been to several of the last 42 games. He is as definitely as nuts as me.

George meets me at my trunk and grabs my 30 lb. table.

"You need help?" he asks, but doesn't wait for a response.

"What are you showing off?" I ask with a smile. "I've been here six weeks, and today is the first day that you help me unload!"

Chris grabs my box of books and delivers them to my spot right under the Apple sign. We exchange our daily pleasantries, and like usual, I tell him that I'll be back in 10 minutes. It's Thursday, which means that it is "roast beef day." George has brought me a roast beef with extra gravy. This is a custom that I have now been included on. The sandwich is good, but being included by the hardest core of the Yankee fans is priceless. I get back into my BMW and laugh to myself as I think, *I could have used some help last month during my bout with hemorrhoids!*

I make a right on 161st and head for The Grand Concourse. This is my 20th day selling books on River Ave. I get pretty lucky as a spot on the right is open. It is a tight fit, but I complete my free parking streak. Twenty for the year and well over 100 home games without paying for parking.

I keep a picture of my dad in the car. It is the laminated Mass card from his funeral. I also look at a picture of Mariano, Kim, Willie and I. I then spend a minute to look at a picture of Jim. "Another day in paradise, Big Guy," I quietly mumble. He was a great guy and I miss him sorely. Sometimes it hits me more than others.

I take a deep breath and wipe away a tear from my right eye. I look in the mirror and smile to myself. Once again, like in 2011, I am proud of myself for having the courage to step out and do something different. Crazy? Yes. Determined? You betcha.

On the drive in, I hear an interview with Michael Kay and Joe Torre. After listening to Joe for a few minutes, I realize how much I miss him, his relaxed demeanor, and how he speaks to reporters. He reminds me of my own father. He is being asked about being the commissioner of baseball. Although he says at 73 he is not the man for the job, he goes on to say how he never felt like he worked a day in his life while he was around baseball.

Do what you love … and the money will follow.

I believe that beginning in March of 2011, I have embarked on a whole new career. I love the Yankees and I love writing. I love doing comedy and making people laugh. I lock the car and begin my daily walk back to River Ave. I can't get the Metallica song out of my head, "Exit light, Enter night ... Off to Never Never Land."

Mixed feelings fill my heart as I am blindsided with emotions.

Some fans cheer. Some fans cry. All the fans know that they are part of something very special. I have been to 60 games this year. I watched as fans from Seattle, Kansas City, Oakland, LA, Tampa, Boston, Baltimore, and Toronto were able to say goodbye. They showered Mariano with gifts and were lavish with their cheers and compliments.

But nothing was like tonight. New York and the fans do it right. It is magical. It is like going to a funeral of a great person, but they are here to feel the love. Nonstop respect is shown for a man who wore the pinstripes and proudly represented the Yankees on and off the field. There is joy and sadness. Sadness that an era of greatness is coming to an end. Joy that we are able to witness it firsthand and see it with our own eyes, hear it with our ears, and feel it to the core of our souls.

With my binoculars, I watch from Section 124. I have a seat three rows back from the Legends section. I sit by myself tonight and watch the drama unfold. In the eighth inning I can see someone warming up. It is a little early for Mo. All of a sudden there is an unmistakable buzz. Cameras began to flash, the outfield box seats and bleachers start to roar. People scramble to get a glimpse and a better angle. I can see without my binoculars that Number 42 is warming up. I notice his typical routine of wind-milling his right arm. The crowd quickly catches on as the cheer started to get louder.

MAH-REE-AHH-NOOOO.

MAH-REE-AHH-NOOOO.

MAH-REE-AHH-NOOOO.

The warm-up tosses begin.

With two on and one out, Joe Girardi begins his slow walk out to the mound. The bullpen door swings open.

The voice of Bob Sheppard rings throughout Yankee Stadium.

"Now pitching, number 42, Mariano Rivera. Number forty-twoooooo."

This will be his 1,115th appearance, 652 of which resulted in saves. For the 576th and final time, the Sandman exits the bullpen and enters the game in front of his home crowd.

Metallica blares to the sellout crowd of 48,675. Everyone who isn't in a wheelchair stands. Some in awe.

The Last 42

Some with tears. All with respect. Cameras flash over and over from the stadium creating a slow motion strobe effect. The Yankees' initial investment of $3,500 more than 20 years ago jogs to the hill in the middle of the diamond.

The Rays team, much like they did for The Captain on July 9, 2011, all stand at the top of the dugout. My mind goes to Jim. He would be watching from his recliner in Melbourne, FL, with his wife Machelle and his dog Jack. He would have been telling his friends and co-workers tomorrow that his little brother was there.

With that a text comes through from my brother Dan.

Wow.

That says it all … even Mets fans are impressed.

The crowd continues to chant.

MAH-REE-AHH-NOOOO.

MAH-REE-AHH-NOOOO.

The first pitch is right back at Mo. He fields it like an infielder and throws the runner out. He quickly gets the third out on a line drive to center. The ovation continues as Rivera makes his way to the dugout. The chant quickly changes from the smart New York crowd.

An-dy Pet-titte.

An-dy Pet-titte.

An-dy Pet-titte.

New York crowds are awesome. They know how to show respect. The chant only gets louder. The Rays stay in the dugout temporarily as they wait for Number 46 to tip his cap. This will be Andy's last curtain call as an active player. In Yankee Stadium it is the ultimate sign of respect.

Andy steps out of the dugout and onto the Yankee Stadium field. The chants grow even louder. Two beloved guys saying goodbye to Yankee Stadium and the fans. One icon would be incredible enough. To have Mo and Andy *both* defies words. It is fitting that Andy and Mo have the two most wins/saves combinations of any two people in history.

Mo receives another ovation as he makes his way for the ninth inning. There are certain moments that you will always remember exactly where you were when they happen.

One out in the ninth. Mariano's 12th pitch of his final home appearance is a cutter that is popped up to 2nd baseman Robinson Cano. Two down in the ninth. This is the moment that we have all been waiting for. Mariano's last out.

Stop the presses. Wait one second. Maybe we just did.

Watching Number 42 play has been one of my greatest thrills

Andy Pettitte and Derek Jeter begin a slow walk out to the mound. Andy signals to the bullpen for the righty as Mariano's face momentarily lights up. It takes him a split second to realize that his teammates and friends of 20 years are taking him out of the game.

Andy reaches the dirt and Mariano collapses into his arms. Booming through the Bronx are the chanting Yankee fans.

MAH-REE-AHH-NOOOO.

MAH-REE-AHH-NOOOO.

MAH-REE-AHH-NOOOO.

The entire Yankee infield is on the mound. Mo stays there and begins to lose it while engulfed in Pettitte's huge embrace. The other Yankees are all gathered on the mound as Jeter looks on in amazement, almost unsure what to do. You can see him mouth the words, "It's OK."

Tears stream down Rivera's face.

"I was bombarded with emotions and feelings that I couldn't describe," Rivera would say later. "Everything hit at that time. I knew that that was the last time."

"He broke down and just gave me a bear hug, and I just bear-hugged him back. He was really crying," Pettitte confessed.

Mo leaves Andy's embrace and falls into the arms of his shortstop. The crowd only gets louder. The YES Network remains silent for a full five minutes as Mariano makes his way back to the dugout. Mariano tips his cap in all directions as he knows that this is it.

Joe Girardi, who served as a teammate, coach, and Mo's second of only two managers, is the first to greet him at the top of the dugout. Mo then takes time to hug every teammate and coach as the crowd continues to cheer.

He embraces A-Rod last. Alex pushes him back out to get one final curtain call from the crowd.

MAH-REE-AHH-NOOOO.

MAH-REE-AHH-NOOOO.

MAH-REE-AHH-NOOOO.

Five straight minutes of cheering for a baseball player who never minded being a role model. A big leaguer who never big-leagued anyone.

The Rays win this one 4-0 but no one seems to care. The normally tough crowd at Yankee Stadium were brought to tears on this last home game of 2013. An era has come to an end. No one in that stadium will ever listen to "Enter Sandman" without thinking of the last 42.

I dodge and maneuver my way around fans to beat them to River Ave. There is not a lot to say but, "Wow." Lots of fist pumps. Lots of tears. Lots of goodbyes. The night isn't over as there is a birthday party for Vinny at the Yankee Tavern. Becki comes over to my table as I set up one last time. Tina The Queen, Udi, and Joel all come to say, "See you in a few months."

I tip my cap to the Bleacher Creatures for their commitment to cheer on their favorite team. For The Creatures, the season is over. I still have a mission to complete, though, and three more meaningless games to attend. Or are they?

Becki comes over and asks me where I am staying in Houston. "I am thinking of coming out there to see Andy's last game," she announces. "I have my postseason money set aside. I might as well use it." Cool. I give her my hotel info and suggest a few airlines. I thank George and Bald Vinny for a great six weeks. I load up my car and watch Yankee Stadium grow smaller in my rearview mirror.

For a few minutes, maybe even a few days, Yankee fans will forget the season that was a major disappointment. It goes to show you, some people are bigger than their circumstances. Saying goodbye to Mariano was more important. Winning championship #28 will have to wait. 2013 was about a different number. It was about saying goodbye to a legend. It was about sending off the last 42 in style.

On the drive back to Long Island, I think about Mo and everything that he has meant to the game of baseball. My mind goes to Derek Jeter. The Core Four no more. Now Jeter is the last man standing. Like most Yankee fans, I contemplate how much longer he will play. I wonder if he will announce his final season in advance like Mo. My fanatical mind wanders. I will already have a streak of 42. If 2014 is the one, I could do his last season and shatter my record of 176 in the process.

My mind is ahead of me. Let's finish this one first.

Friday, September 27

At 7:00 a.m., I get dropped off by Danny and Annie for my final road trip of 2013.

We talk about the last few months. Being around family and staying with Danny and Maureen is one of the things that made it so special. We all live on average 28,000 days. My last 45 have been spent with my family, the Yankees, and their fans. What could be better than that?

We discuss last night and how powerful it was. Danny, Moe, and Annie have probably watched every game over the last six weeks. Danny will be traveling when I get back from Houston and I thank him for a great six weeks.

The Last 42 have come down to the last three. As I wait to board my flight, I get an email from one of Jim's former students.

> *Dear members of Mr. Melia's family,*
>
> *I know you probably don't know me, but my name is Scott Adams and I graduated with the class of 2013 from West Shore. Mr. Melia and I had an incredibly close relationship, which is something that I will miss, cherish, and look back on for the rest of my life. I know that you and all of his family have heard how he impacted everyone he met in a positive way from close friends and people he worked with, but not from a student, which is why I am writing to you today.*
>
> *When I first heard the news of what happened to Mr. Melia I didn't want to believe it. I could not believe that a man who was my best friend at the school was gone. The thought of not being able to*

see him in person, hear his voice, talk to him, joke with him, visit him when I'm back from college, and most importantly, not be able to thank him for all he did for me crushed me inside. I know you don't know this, but Mr. Melia was way more than just a dean or assistant principal to me. He was a friend that would joke with me in between classes, always ask me how the basketball season was going, and growing up with some problems in my life he was always there for me when I needed someone to talk too. He was a man that changed my life and I am forever thankful.

When I came to West Shore in 9th grade I could care less about getting good grades and was someone who lived to get in trouble. If I would have stayed on this track it would have led to me being kicked out of West Shore, going to Melbourne High School, and continuing on the same track leading to me not being accepted to college and a poor start in life. Thanks to Mr. Melia, this did not happen. Every day he would check in on me asking how my grades were doing, if I was staying out of trouble, and how I was in general. I don't know what it was but he saw something in me, some kind of potential that gave him the drive to go out of his way every day to make sure that I was doing well.

When he first started these little checks on me I didn't really strive to do better and did not see what he was doing for me. I was ignorant and now wish I would have listened to him sooner. However, one day near the end of my freshman year he said something to my mom that spoke to me and really gave me a push in the right direction. He said, "You know Beth, one of two things are going to happen. Either Scott is going to fail out of West Shore, go to Mel High, and not succeed academically, or he is going to get his act together and four years from now you'll see him walk across the stage, shake my hand, receive his high school diploma, and soon after be off to college." When my mom told me these words he said, it left me stunned there for a second rethinking everything I had been doing the last couple years. Thanks to Mr. Melia, I realized what I was doing was wrong and in order to succeed in life I needed to stay at West Shore and begin to do well.

Now, four years later, I am exactly where Mr. Melia envisioned me being my freshman year. I graduated from high school, got accepted to University of North Florida, and now just finished my summer term receiving an A in World History. There isn't a person I can give more credit too than Mr. Melia. Without him, none of this would have happened and who knows where I would be today. All I know is that I am incredibly thankful and just wish more than anything that I could speak to him one last time and thank him for all he has done. Thinking back to graduation day, I never ever would have thought that that would be the last day I'd see him. After graduating, I thought about when I'd come back to West Shore to see the basketball games and be able to catch up with him and joke with him just as we did the years prior. It makes me terribly sad that this won't happen and that when I go to the basketball games from now on, he will not be there. However, I know if Mr. Melia was here to talk to me right now, he would want me to look at the bright side of what has happened and that is what I plan on trying to do.

Even though my dear friend and mentor has passed on, I like to think about it as if we all now have an angel watching over us who will guide us in the right direction throughout life until the day we join him. Whenever I step on campus, he is going to be the man I think of. Whenever I go into the basketball gym I am going to see him standing by the entrance where he once always stood. Whenever I see a golf cart I am going to remember all the times he would drive me around campus on it. Whenever I think of the Wildcat Nation, I am going to remember that he did all he could for us, and whenever I think about the successes I have in my life I am going to remember and thank Mr. Melia because without him it wouldn't have happened.

The crazy thing is it wasn't only me who had this kind of close relationship with Mr. Melia, all the students did. Mr. Melia was a friendly, comforting, funny, nice, and all around amazing man who touched the lives of everyone he knew. I know all the students including myself feel truly blessed to have known such a remarkable man and I'm beyond thankful to have had the blessing of him helping me throughout the last four years. I truly believe that even though Mr. Melia is not physically here anymore, his spirit will always be helping everyone he

> knew just as he did before. Your family was truly blessed for having such a great man in your life and I hope that you can share this story with other close relatives and friends of Mr. Melia to show that he was truly appreciated and loved by the students. We will miss him more than words can explain and he will never be forgotten.

Scott's email is the true godsend, and well-timed as I head into this home stretch. It reminds me anew why I am doing this — to honor a great baseball player and to honor the memory of a great human being — my brother, Jim.

A few minutes later, I am on Jet Blue and watch SportsCenter over and over. This is the first time that I get to witness the replay of Andy and Jete taking Mo out of the game. I can't get enough of it.

I get up to go the bathroom in the back of the plane. I grab a *162* book and think of my new friend, Becki, and her random acts of kindness. I met a father and his son before we boarded. They are headed to Houston for the final three games. That is cool. His name is Galen, and his son, who is about 8, is named Cilus. I hand them a book.

"I thought you guys would enjoy this," I say. The father's eyes light up as he tells his son to say thank you.

Thank Becki, I think to myself. Becki does stuff for the sake of doing them. I do them because it feels good and

I hope that it will lead to future sales or book promotion.

As I wait for the bathroom to open up, I see him passing my book around and telling the *162* story. "That guy went to every Yankee game in 2011. He is the author."

I arrive in Houston to an overcast day and little fanfare. I check in at the DoubleTree downtown, about a mile from Minute Maid Park. I cross off another ballpark that I have attended as I make way into the stadium. I move up to the first row down the right field line.

With the Yankees clinging to a healthy lead toward the end of the game, David Robertson is warming up. I can't believe it. Fans have flown in from all over to see Rivera's final pitches and in a save situation they go to Robertson?

I feel myself getting worked up. For six weeks I have been waiting for this moment. I don't get it. Robertson comes in and gets the save. The future Yankees closer will have plenty of opportunities soon. It's hard to rack up saves when you have Mariano in the bullpen a few feet away. But why are they using him *now*?

We find out shortly afterwards why Mo didn't pitch.

"I don't have any more bullets left," he confessed. "My tank is empty."

In fact, Mo shares that he has been pitching in pain much of the last few months. He had to go in for some heat treatment in between innings on Thursday. He also shares that he wants his last memory to be the one at Yankee Stadium. Although I am disappointed and wanted to see the man one more time, I get it. He's done.

Saturday, Sept 28

Today will be about watching Andy Pettitte close out his career. I am glad that I'm in Texas to witness it. Andy has lived in Houston for years, so this is a fitting goodbye.

The game tonight is at 6 p.m. and my Rockstar package is set for 3:45-5:45. My local contact and LegalShield Regional Manager is Lyncee Schuman. She is a native New Yorker and was happy to set up the trip. We have never met in person, but she was happy to be heading up my final stop. She even arranged for me to have tickets on Friday night.

Ashley and I take the shuttle and arrive before most of the fans today. We walk into the same bar that we closed the night before and it is time to do some magic. I introduce myself to the bar manager and let her know

There is Crying in Baseball

that I have 25 people coming and I am planning on doing a book signing. They want to put me upstairs on the third level.

I fell for this once in Tampa and talk my way into being able to set up right at the entrance. There is a big Budweiser canopy booth that is usually used for selling beers when the bar is slammed. The owner tells me that they usually use it for special promotions, but welcomes me to set up a *162* booth. Nice.

As I set up, a gentleman in a wheelchair is watching me.

"What are you selling?"

I briefly stop, walk over, and hand him a baseball card. "I'm the 162 guy," I announce.

As I have hundreds of times in the last 44 days, I tell him my story. If you share a good idea often enough, it will fall on the right ears.

The man's name is Bill and he is a longtime Houstonian. He is wearing a Colt 45's jersey. We continue to chat as I set up and he fills me in on the history of the organization. I didn't know that The Colt 45's were ever a team. It doesn't take long for his wife to wander over and buy him a birthday present. My mom always told me that it is nice to be nice. Many of my book sales this year and have come from just engaging in conversation and being friendly.

The first Rockstar to arrive is Rory Lane. Rory, who is a motivational speaker and a part-time LegalShield associate steps up to my makeshift bar and I hand him his ticket and sign a book for him. As I do that, two Yankee fans line up behind him. One wants to know about the book and the other tries to order two Miller Lights.

Lyncee shows up with a case of my books and a list of Rockstars. She is a natural networker and works the crowd as I sign books. She is friendly, pleasant, and makes my job easy today. I flash back to the fiasco in Tampa and how I oversold the package.

To make the Rockstar package work, I have to buy the cheapest seats possible. Today we are seated in 433, which is about four miles from homeplate. The good news is that Andy continues his dominant pitching from last weekend. After five innings, the Yanks are down 1-0. Pettitte has only thrown 65 pitches. He is electric. The Yankees put two on the scoreboard in the sixth to go ahead 2-1.

I am itching to move up, but do not want to be rude. Aww, hell with it. In the sixth, I announce that I'm going to move down in a bit. After the third out in the bottom of the sixth, we gather for a group picture and I make a quick escape.

We use our Sunday tickets, thanks to Jimmy Jenkins, to get into Section 132. Remember, they *never* look at the date, only at the section. Ashley and Jorge Tobar, my friend who flew in from Arizona, are trying to keep up. They are very timid as we continue to make our way down. We pass open seat after open seat. I can tell that they are both thinking, *OK, this is good!*

I have my yellow sign and I want to get as close as possible. This one reads: *Andy and Mo - The CLASS of 2013*. There are four seats open in the very front row off of the right field line. We have all of our stuff, so it is difficult to look like we belong there.

We sit and I introduce myself to the guy on my left, who is decked out in Astros garb.

He gives us a look that says, "What are you guys doing here?" I know that I must win him over fast, or we will be getting kicked out of these sick seats.

"You guys big baseball fans?" I inquire to get the ball rolling.

"Yeah I've had these seats for years," he remarks with a hint of pride, but also frustration with the Astros who possess the worst record in baseball. I hold up a copy of *162*.

"So check this out. I'm an author and I just finished a book signing before the game. I have a few extra copies, I'd like to give you one."

His demeanor changes immediately. He opens up telling me that his name is Marc and I encourage him to live his dreams, as I do with every book that I sign. He begins to show *162* around and is telling everyone within earshot about my journey. I have a new friend and an enthusiastic promoter. A fan in the row behind asks how much, as I sell another book.

We all stand for "God Bless America" and "Take Me Out to the Ballgame." Marc and his friend to the left keep firing away questions. Both of their bodies are turned more towards me than homeplate.

In the top of the 8th, Robinson Cano slaps the ball quickly down the line. Because I was carrying so many books today, and mainly because our "real" seats were in the nosebleeds, I opted to leave my glove at the DoubleTree. Wouldn't you know it, the ball is coming right at us.

I have my Bud Light bottle in one hand and can't decide how to play this. We are right over the wall and the ground is just a few feet away. Marc, on my left, uses quick thinking and his Astros hat to swipe at the ball. It goes into his hat and bounces out, rolling a few feet away.

I see the first base umpire looking our way as he stands on the outer edge of the infield. He grabs his wrist above his head. Uh oh. Apparently that is the signal that spectator interference has occurred.

By definition: *When a spectator or other person not associated with one of the teams (including such staff as bat boys or ball girls) alters play in progress, it is spectator interference. Such interference often occurs when a spectator in the first row of seats reaches onto the field to attempt to grab a fair or foul fly ball. If the umpire judges that the fielder could have caught the ball over the field (i.e., the ball would have not crossed over the plane of the wall), he will rule the batter out on spectator interference. Also, the spectator who commits interference is usually ejected from the stadium.*

Oh, jeesh.

I suddenly realize that the ball was live. This means the ball is fair and Marc has interfered with the game and Cano is awarded second base. Interesting.

Authorities arrive within seconds. The security guard looks right at me as he leans down and asks "Did you touch that ball with your hat?" I shake my head no and hold up my hands showing my innocence. I am wearing my FDNY hat but it never came off of my head. The on-field security guard is looking at me as well. He speaks into his walkie-talkie.

"OK. I'll ask again," he says sternly. "Who stopped that ball?"

Marc meekly raises his hand.

"OK, you need to come upstairs with us."

He gathers his beer, his autographed *162* book, and is escorted away. It's a good thing I didn't have my glove. I'm sure that I would have out reached past his trusty Astros hat. The funny reality is that the three of us were so engrossed in a conversation that we just weren't paying attention. None of us realized that it was a live ball.

I get a text from back in the Bronx from Udi.

Just saw you on YES. Did you touch that ball?? You ARE a nut!

Jorge, Ashley, and I think it is hysterical that a Houston season ticket holder just got ejected. I give Marc credit for being honest, because it was me that they were coming after. The on-field security guard revisits me after the third Yankee out.

"We looked at the replay. We believe that you are the one who touched that ball." He is grinning big as he says it.

"No way," is all that I can muster up.

I sort of wish that it *was* me, as it would have made a great story. Except that I would have missed Andy's final pitches. And on this night, Andy is simply marvelous. As the innings roll by, I keep my eye on the scoreboard for his pitch count. Ninety-two pitches after seven innings. As legendary broadcaster Chris Berman says, "He could go all — the — way!"

Well, he can go at least into the 8th. After a 1-2-3 eighth inning, I figure that Girardi would bring him in for at least one batter so he could get a nice ovation from his hometown crowd.

Being part of Andy Pettitte's final game of his career is amazing. It goes to show you that it takes a team. Teamwork makes the dream work. Andy, Mo, Jeter, Jorge Posada, Bernie Williams, Tino Martinez, Paulie O'Neill, and David Cone can all look at their careers and know it was the team that always made them stronger. Andy and Mo were a huge part of each other's careers. To have them saying goodbye together is very special.

The fans stand in anticipation for every pitch in the ninth. From my seat in the front row I try to engage the crowd. I start an "An-dy Pet-titte" chant several times, but no one else joins in. Where are The Creatures when you need them?

Marc is missing a great ending to a Hall of Fame career. Andy retires the second batter as well. Girardi is going to let him finish.

Not so fast, as Chris Carter slaps a single.

Pettitte is at 114 pitches. With the score 2-1, Girardi comes out to the mound to a chorus of boos. The fans want to see Pettitte finish this one. What are you saving him for? Girardi barely makes it to the mound before quickly turning back for the dugout. The boos turn into cheers. Andy wants to finish this one.

Michael Kay on YES Network called the last play:

> The 1-0 from Pettitte. Grounder to third. This could be it. Nunez across the diamond. Yankees win 2-1. And Andy Pettitte completes his career with a complete game. What a way to go. He had not had a complete game since 2006; he is the oldest starting pitcher in baseball. In the 161st game of the Yankee season he spins a complete game to end his career, in just the perfect manner.
>
> And the crowd chanting "Andy Pettitte," here just miles from his hometown of Deer Park. What a way to end it. Andy finishes his career on a high note. Now he is the only pitcher in big league history to pitch over 15 years and not have a losing season. So he evens his record at 11-11. And what a way for him to go out. Yankee fans and Texans saying thank you. The oldest starting pitcher in baseball says goodbye.

There it is. The perfect ending. This again will go down

as one of my top moments as a sports fan.

The Yankee rush out of the dugout to congratulate their teammate. As usual, Derek Jeter is one of the first to reach Andy and give him a huge hug. Mariano is right before him with his big Panamanian smile.

An on-field security guard, also named Mark, comes over again and tells me that they have reviewed the video and I was the one who touched the ball. I laugh him off and say, "Nice try. You got the right guy." He has a big smile and certainly is friendly.

I pull out one of the few *162* books that I have left and autograph a copy.

"You coming tomorrow? I'll take care of you," he says.

We make our way back to the bar and I set up my books again. Fans buy stuff when their team wins or when something big happens. Well, no playoffs this year and no more Mariano, but something amazing happened today. Andy Pettitte threw his final pitch. Just like in Da Bronx, they are buying.

A Yankees fan named Lenny is speaking with Ashley. "This is him," she says pointing at me. "He wrote the book."

"You know Bald Vinny?" he asks.

I point at the cover. "He did my foreword. In fact I

have been set up with my books with him since mid-August."

"How did I miss you? I was just at his birthday party on Thursday!" he says.

"I was there, too, at the Yankee Tavern!"

Lenny forks over $15 as his friends are trying to pry him away and make it to another bar. He stays a few more minutes and we chat about Mo and Andy and the Yankees' uncertain future.

Sunday, September 29

All Good Things Must Come to an End.

I convince a hung-over Jorge and Ashley to leave early and see if the Yankees are having batting practice. Several thousand fans had the same idea and the area surrounding the Yankee dugout is nearly impossible to get to.

Two young kids are signing autographs. It takes me a minute, but I realize that they are Rivera's two boys. No other Yankees are on the field. We make our way to pretty decent seats behind homeplate. I have a seat right behind the Yankee dugout to take in the final of *The Last 42* ceremonies.

I immediately spot former skipper Joe Torre who is

dressed sharply in a suit. I then notice a really big guy wearing jeans and a Texas Longhorns hat. It takes me a split second to realize who it is. Jeter leaps out of the dugout and gives him a huge hug.

Mariano makes his first entrance of the day as he races out to see The Rocket, Roger Clemens. Joe Torre is the first one introduced as he shares what it was like to manage for George Steinbrenner. He references Andy Pettitte's masterpiece from last night and the crowd erupts. He also speaks of how blessed he was to be able to manage special players like Derek Jeter.

He then gives a glowing recap of working with Mariano Rivera.

"I started managing the Yankees in 1996 and I was there for 12 years," Torre said. "Trust me, you don't get a chance to manage for George Steinbrenner for 12 years unless you have someone like this coming out of the bullpen."

"When somebody came into our clubhouse who came from another team or from the Minor Leagues and looked like he was out of place somewhat, Mariano would go over and put his arm around him," Torre said. "Players were made to feel welcome by Mo.

The thing I'm going to miss now when I'm watching games is the fact that you always tuned in to watch Mariano when he ran out of that bullpen. Every single player that he played with has been touched in a positive way.

"You never have to worry about dialing the wrong number when you called the bullpen. The five rings definitely wouldn't have been possible without Mo."

The announcer then brings up the seven-time Cy Young winner and winner of more than 350 games, Roger Clemens. I cheer loudly as I recall some fond memories rooting for Number 22 during his two stops in NY. They played together from 1999-03 and again in 2007. His reception is mixed as many in the crowd boo him more loudly than I cheer.

So much for southern hospitality.

As a Yankees fan and fan of Mo, I know that Clemens was a huge part of our dynasty and I was always a little more excited when he took the mound. Mike, Kim, and I flew out for game four of the World Series in Miami in 2003. It was supposed to be his last time pitching.

Dressed in his jeans and wearing his hat with his sunglasses on top, he looks more like Kenny Powers, the fictional character from the HBO television series "Eastbound & Down." Whether it is his out-of-place wardrobe or his lackluster reception, the Rocket looks nervous and fumbles over his words.

"Mariano, I'm going to make this short and sweet." He proceeds to tell Mo what an honor it was to play with him.

"Incredible," Clemens said. "Incredible person, incredible teammate. Nobody wants to see him go. There are not many sure things in this world. But when we saw you coming in from [the bullpen], that's as close as you're going to get."

Then Mariano comes out and trumps all of his other classy moves.

"I want to make sure to apologize to the Houston Astros players and the great fans in Houston, because I couldn't compete my last three days of the season," he said. "I apologize for that. I want to leave with the game I played at Yankee Stadium on Thursday — I want to keep that memory of mine. For that, I apologize. You guys deserved more, but I'm being a little selfish."

My disappointment from the weekend quickly fades as I am reminded why Mariano is so beloved. He is real and he never puts himself above anyone else. Ever. His record for saves will remain at 652. His record for ERA will stay at 2.19. His reputation for doing and saying the right thing will remain untarnished. His goal of never big-leaguing anyone remains unblemished.

The perfect ending.

Exit light. Enter Night. Off to Never Never Land.

Game 162, and the last of my Last 42 tour, will go down as one of the most boring games I have ever been to. We spend much of the time checking football scores. The Yanks are down 1-0, but tie the game in the top of the 8th. I joke that if it goes into extra innings, who knows, we may see Mo after all.

My theory gets tested as the game does just that. In the top of the 14th, with many of the fans already on the highway or home watching the Broncos-Eagles game, Mark Reynolds slams a tie-breaking homerun. The Bombers add a few more and we head for the exit.

I'll always remember these 42 special games that Jim and I were able to attend together. Two brothers with one mission: Close out the career of the greatest closer and arguably one of the greatest men who have ever lived. For 45 days, Jim and I did something special. We didn't even annoy each other. We definitely didn't fight. Our Mom would have been proud.

I've learned some valuable lessons: Be more like Mo. Smile more. Listen more intently. Be more patient with others. Treat everyone like they matter. Never big-league anyone. Be more like Becki. Practice more random acts of kindness. Be generous and do good. Getting a ball is nice, but *giving* a ball to a kid that you'll never see again is priceless. Make time for everyone and make everyone count, like Bald Vinny.

These are the same lessons that Jim left the world.

There is Crying in Baseball

Life is short. Make the choice to enjoy it.

Epilogue

Thursday, June 16, 2016

Realizing that it has been almost two years since my last entry, I realized that an updating was in order for those who might need closure on some loose ends in the story.

I just got off the phone with my nephew, Matt, and I have never been more proud or respected him more than I do today. Like many of us, he struggled and he stumbled several times but he kept moving forward. Matt went through a second stint of rehab in November of 2014 and has been clean and sober ever since.

Today, he is becoming the leader that he was destined to be as he currently sponsors five others who are battling their addictions. He told me tonight that he stays clean for them as much as for himself. The addict becomes the teacher. The tipping point.

With Matt and Mary. I'm so proud of the man he's becoming.

He is also overcoming his fear of public speaking as he travels the southeast to conferences and events sharing his journey. I love him so much and I'm proud of him for changing — and probably saving his life.

I saw my daughter Macie Grace this week. We have an open adoption and we get to see each other every few months. She turned 2½ last month. I feel so blessed to still have the opportunity to watch her grow up and be part of her life. She has changed my life and I strive to be a better person so as we continue to grow closer she will look up to me.

The adoptive family are the most amazing, loving peo-

Epilogue

ple in the world and do everything to facilitate Macie Grace and I having a relationship. I am forever grateful. Although I believe I will always feel the pain of guilt for giving up my baby, I truly believe that this was the best life for her. She is so loved and so happy with her parents and two brothers. I hope that when she is old enough to read this that she knows that I love her more than life itself and would do anything for her. I hope she understands. I think of her and miss her every day.

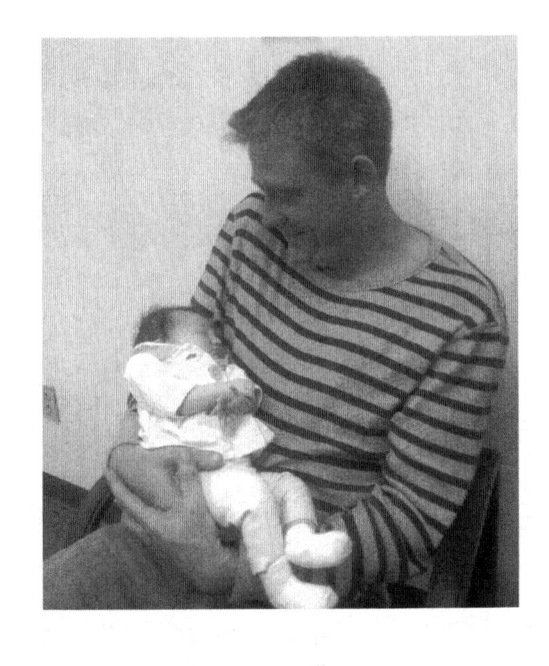

Tragedy hit the Melia family again in May of 2015, as we lost my godson and nephew, Timmy Melia. Tim was a decorated U.S. Marine who served two tours in Iraq and vigorously fought for his country. He was also a brave member of the FDNY. Tim, 30, left behind his wife Lisa and their four children Madison, Desiree, Chloe, and little Timmy. We all miss him every day.

It's been almost three years since we lost Jim and I took

my *Last 42* journey. I think it took me so long to write the story because it brings closure to something that I don't want closure to. I've procrastinated long enough.

I may never understand or know why Jim was taken from us at such a young age. But I do know that he made the world a better place and, he is missed by so many of us.

What I learned from both Jim and Tim is that life is short and we should appreciate every moment that we have with those we love. It was also greatly reinforced that we must all live our dreams. Nothing is guaranteed, but anything is possible.

Remember the dash. Make your life count.

Jim and Tim Melia both did.

About the Author

Steve Melia is an author, comedian, network marketer, philanthropist and a baseball fanatic.

Steve attended all 162 NY Yankees games in 2011 and wrote his first book *162: The Almost Epic of a Yankees Superfan* (2013).

Steve has been an independent associate with LegalShield since 1998 and along with his partners Mike and Kim Melia have built one of the largest direct sales forces within the company. He currently serves as the Regional General Manager of California, Hawaii, and Nevada.

Steve is a highly sought-after inspirational speaker and travels extensively using sports and humor to relate to audiences. He has been doing stand up comedy since 2008.

Steve, Mike, and Kim are affectionately known as The Melia Family and founded Work, Play, Love, which is an organization that supports orphanages and children in Guatemala.

Steve recently launched "The 162 Experience" podcast with fellow sports fanatic Benito Armenta. The podcast is about success in business, sports, and life.

Steve Makes his home in San Diego, California. He can be reached at meliacomedy@gmail.com.